England before Elizabeth

ENGLAND
BEFORE
ELIZABETH

Helen Cam

Professor of History Emerita, Harvard
University, Fellow of Girton College,
Cambridge

HARPER TORCHBOOKS   The Academy Library

HARPER & ROW, PUBLISHERS, NEW YORK

To
M. G. J. AND F. S.

ACKNOWLEDGMENT

Whilst my debt to numberless scholars must of necessity go unacknowledged, I should like here to express my gratitude to Professor Dorothy Whitelock for giving me the quotations from Anglo-Saxon literature on pages 24 and 38. My obligations to Professor David Knowles in regard to Chapter XI go beyond the printed word.

CONTENTS

There is a saying known of yore,
    What is a kingdom's treasury?
Cattle and beasts, corn stuffed in store,
    Rich commons and wise clergy;
    Merchants, squires, chivalry
That will be ready at need to rise;
    And a chivalrous king, of wisdom high,
To lead in war and govern in peace.
                    (*English Poem of* 1401)

INTRODUCTION

'Look unto the rock whence ye are hewn and to
the hole of the pit whence ye are digged.'

THE Middle Ages are to many men more remote than
classical times. For such the word medieval is synonymous
with archaic, and they will only wish to read its history if the
romance of remoteness attracts them, that timeless yet catastrophic quality, those 'strong passions, enormous crimes, and
profound superstitions,' which led the youthful Disraeli to
choose the thirteenth century as the background for his tragedy
in 1839. The romanticism of the Middle Ages is as fictitious as the
modernity of the classical age, our knowledge of which we owe,
incidentally, to the medieval scholars whose 'monkish Latin'
is so barbarous and ugly to the 'classical' Latinist.

The first claim the Middle Ages makes on our interest is
that of piety. We owe so much to it; the men of the Middle
Ages transmitted to us both the learning of the pre-Christian
ages and the civilization of Christianity. Over and above that
they had their own gifts to give us, and in this country before
all others it is our medieval ancestors who have made us what
we are. We have never broken the living links which bind us to
them; their words, their thoughts, their habits, are ours; they
have set their stamp on our roads, our fields, our hedges, our
districts, on our buildings and our building, on our laws and
our law.

Our parliament, once the subject for envious admiration
amongst 'less happier lands,' later regarded with supercilious
disdain, recognized to-day as a plant of native growth, that
refuses to breed true when removed from its peculiar environment, owes not only its origin but its character to the
men of the Middle Ages.

The Church of England, equally unique and equally
inexplicable, can no more than parliament be explained by the
wily masterfulness of the Tudors or the exigencies of the

ix

sixteenth century. Henry VIII and Elizabeth were master workmen, but both their materials and their tools had been prepared for them through the centuries that came before.

As Boniface said of the Old Saxons eleven hundred years ago, when he called on his home country of Wessex for a great missionary effort, so we can say of medieval Englishmen: "they are our blood and our bone." But in recognizing this essential unity, we must not try to force them into a twentieth-century pattern.

It is the likeness in difference that constitutes the special charm of chasing hares in a medieval forest. The fact that little William Marshall played 'conkers' with King Stephen in 1141 as children play it to-day, or that he was a hostage, only differing from the hostages of the Gestapo in that his jailers had kind hearts, or that his standards of conduct for the decent Christian were not precisely those of the clergy, must not lead us to assume that a child's life or a gentleman's code in the twelfth century can be understood without some effort of the imagination and some detachment from the assumptions of the twentieth century. We recognize the human attitude as familiar to us; we must not attempt to explain society or government in the light of the theories and assumptions of to-day any more than we should attempt to explain Socrates or Cicero in terms of a Christian philosophy.

The story we have to trace is that of the evolution of the English nation—the amalgamation of differing races and the unification of warring tribal princedoms into one monarchy under the stress of competition for power, the disciplinary influence of Christianity, the stimulus of foreign invasion, the compression of conquest, the centralization of government, the standardization of institutions, the interchange of trade, and the triumph of one common tongue in the rivalry of languages and dialects.

Of the forces making for unity, after the sea 'which serves it in the office of a wall,' and the challenge from without in the days of the Vikings, the strongest have been kingship and law. In kingship were focused the ancient tribal tradition of the leadership of the folk; the loyalty and love owed by a man to his lord, common to Anglo-Saxon, Dane, Norman, and Angevin; and, most significant of all, the aspirations towards justice cherished by the Christian Church. In the oath by which the archbishop bound the king at his coronation to see that justice was done to all, lies the warranty for the ever-growing activities of royal government; the assumption of fresh duties, and the devising of new means for discharging them. The sword of justice, carried before him at his coronation, is the symbol of that executive power which was unquestionably his, and without which the established rights of his subjects might be of no effect.

But even more ancient and more persistent was the force of law: the ancient law of the folk, older than the king, preserved in the memory of men before the days of written records, declared by the country-side, made effective by the power of the crown and the wisdom of the king's skilled servants, and yet, as Magna Carta declared, above the king.

It was guarded by the uprightness and independence of the judges, the best of whom, like Sir Thomas More, knew themselves to be 'the king's servants, but God's first.' Local at first, it became common to all England as the monarchy took over responsibility for enforcing and improving it, its forms multiplying to meet the demands of a growing and expanding society. It showed itself able to absorb in turn the Frankish jury that kept alive the old English responsibility of the neighbourhood, the equitable processes that enabled new contractual and commercial relationships to be adequately protected, and the Roman *lèse-majesté* that expanded the feudal offence of treason against a lord into the crime of the individual against the nation state.

No one can be at home in medieval England unless he recognizes the universal belief in law as sanctioning the rights of all men, and of justice as exercised by the highest and wisest members of the community, whether Alfred the Great or St. Louis or Chief Justice Gascoigne—men who had the fear of God before their eyes and unquestioningly accepted the ultimate principles of right and wrong, and were prepared to bend their energies to applying those principles to the complex and varying problems of human rights and wrongs. To kingship at the top corresponded the common man's indefeasible property in the common law of England, his from time immemorial—shared even by the unfree as regarded his life and limb, though not his liberty; extended to every man as serfdom died out.

'To make of many peoples one commonwealth, what means are surer or more fitting, what bond stronger or worthier, than the following of common customs and of equal laws?'

CHAPTER I

BRITAIN BEFORE THE ENGLISH

(1) PRE-ROMAN BRITAIN

THE first common and continuing factors in our history are the physical attributes of our island. Whilst its position on the extreme edge of the Eurasian land mass has delayed the impact of the forces that came from the Continent, its deeply indented coast line, its good harbours, and the narrowness and shallowness of the seas that separate it from Europe have made it exceedingly vulnerable.

From the period, approximately seven thousand years ago, when the steady process of subsidence allowed the waters of the North Sea to break the landbridge that joined Britain to the Continent, traders and invaders alike have of necessity been water borne. The small capacity of sailing vessels in early times, and the delay imposed by a sea voyage meant that invaders could only reach us in small contingents and the penetration was slow; and thus the successive waves of different cultures broke on the island in different ripples rather than in overwhelming breakers, and (the new-comers blended with those already there instead of submerging them. In the long run this has produced the most mongrel of all people.) As Defoe said, the 'true-born Englishman' is:

'A metaphor invented to express
A man that's kin to all the universe.'

Again, our climate, ranging in prehistoric times from tropical to glacial, has, probably as the result of the free circulation of Atlantic currents round our shores, settled into one whose unpredictability exacts constant extemporization and adjustment, but whose moist and temperate character has encouraged the steady advance of pasture and agriculture.

The history of colonization in Britain has been the encroachment of the herd and the plough upon the woodland which once covered all the lower levels of the island, chalk downs as well as limestone uplands. It has been said that the desert has made Islam the natural creed of the Arab, and the steppes and the forest created the Russian character; it can hardly be questioned that the millennia of persistent and rewarding labour upon the soil of Britain have produced ingrained habits of enterprise, of pertinacity, and of gradualism in the inhabitants of the island.

The first cultivators of the soil came from the south-west. By a process of expansion rather than invasion they advanced from the Mediterranean by way of Spain, reaching our island somewhere about 2500 B.C., and they have left the memorial of the centuries of their dominion in their great stone communal graves—cairns and long barrows—scattered over the Scottish Highlands, Ireland, Man, Wales, and south-west England. They were traders and farmers; they pursued agriculture and kept flocks; they practised weaving and pottery. They mined gold and tin, but for their harder implements they still used finely worked stone for many centuries, until they learned the technique of blending Irish copper with Cornish tin, and began to exploit the uses of bronze.

By this time another series of waves of immigration from the East, from about 1900 B.C. onwards, had brought to the eastern parts of the island the people whose 'curious and distinctive drinking pots' have given them with the learned the name of the Beaker Folk; a more war-like race, ready to seize on the advantages of bronze for their tools and weapons, less settled in habit, being more given to pasture than to agriculture.

It is with the arrival of the Beaker Folk that the effects of another physical feature of our island begin to be traceable: its geological structure. As J. R. Green pointed out, the uplands of southern Britain are in the form of a hand, with Salisbury Plain as the palm, from which radiate the South Downs as the little finger, the North Downs as the ring finger, the Berkshire Downs, Chilterns and East Anglian heights as the middle finger; the Cotswolds, the Midland uplands, and the Lincoln heights as the forefinger, with the Welsh mountains as the thumb. To immigrants coming from the east the chalk and limestone uplands were the natural lines of advance, and the most promising regions for settlement. The marshy, densely wooded lower levels of the river valleys had clays too stiff for their implements of cultivation; the downs and wolds were more easily cleared, excellent for grazing and corn-growing.

It has been said that 'God made the country, but man made the town.' The antithesis is imperfect, if not false. There are few rural landscapes, however wild, that are not marked by man's hand, by clearing or hedge or wall or dyke; above all by path or road. Men walk where others have walked, and while the cultivated fields of our fore-runners may relapse to the wild, and be only discernible by the airman's eye, and the beakers of the Beaker Folk may await the skilled exhumation of the archæologist, the way they walked and the way their beasts walked may direct the steps of others thousands of years later.

The Icknield Way that first served the purposes of the Bronze Age trader was used by the Anglo-Saxon, the Danish, and the Norman invaders as it is by the motorist of to-day. Like the less well-known Harroway,[1] that runs from Canterbury to Salisbury, it formed part of a road system that converged on Salisbury Plain, the commercial and religious centre of the Beaker Folk. Where the Iberians from the south had worshipped the earth mother in secret chambers, they worshipped the sky god in temples open to the sunlight—Stonehenge, Avebury, and the lesser hilltop circles.

For some five hundred years, roughly from 1500 to 1000 B.C., a distinctive island culture was being established by the gradual blending of the two traditions that had come from the west and from the east, reinforced by more immigrants who extended trading connections, and carried the arts of architecture and craftsmanship in gold and bronze yet further in conditions of comparative peace and prosperity.

[1]Miscalled by pseudo-antiquarians the Pilgrim's Way.

The exquisite craftsmanship and artistic design of the hand-mirrors, brooches, bracelets, necklaces, helmets, harness-fittings, sword scabbards, and shields of this period displays, in its 'wild delicacy,' the local variation of the European tradition that takes its name from La Tène. In the pottery of the Glastonbury Lake Village, in the Aylesford mask, and in the White Horse of Uffington we can trace that genius for linear decoration which we meet again in the *Book of Kells* and other work of Anglo-Irish inspiration. It is with those who made and used such beautiful objects, and many others more perishable, and who were sophisticated enough to use cogged dice, that we should associate pre-Roman Britain, not with mythical savages dyed in woad and dressed in skins.

Travellers' tales of the island were, in fact, being told in the Mediterranean countries that had acquired the habit of writing. By the time of Alexander the Great it was being called by a name recognizably like Britain, and as contacts became more frequent, its inhabitants were recognized as akin to the Gauls—those Celtic peoples who had been pressing in on the Balkan and Italian peninsulas from the fourth century B.C. onwards, had sacked the little town of Rome about 387 B.C., and were the dominant race in Transalpine Gaul when Roman expansion carried the eagles west of the Alps and northwards from the Mediterranean. There is thus external written evidence for the movement of the last body of immigrants on Britain—the Belgae—who arrived here about 75 B.C.

With the Belgae came the first indirect touch of Teutonic influence, for they came from the heavier forest lands of Northern Europe, and brought with them better iron tools than had yet been known here, and a plough which made possible the first determined attack on the stiff clays of the river valleys of southern Britain; soil far more productive for grain than the uplands, but impossible for a 'scratch' agriculture to exploit.

This cultivation of the lower levels entails a descent from the uplands, and a consequent re-orientation of the whole pattern of settlement. Not only do sites like those of Winchester and Chichester replace the hill-top 'British camps' as tribal centres. The towns of Verulam (St. Albans) and Camulodunum

(Colchester), founded by the Belgic line of warrior princes who asserted themselves as the dominant power in Southern Britain in the century before the Roman conquest, are significant of a change in the balance of importance; the south-east rather than the south-west was in future to be the economic and strategic centre of Britain. Cymbeline's capital at Colchester had its mint and its wharves on the Colne, where pottery and other goods from Gaul were unloaded, and corn and slaves and hunting dogs were shipped for export to the Continent.

But the economic and political ascendancy that the house of Cymbeline exercised over the other tribes of southern Britain was not of a kind that would be able to stand up against an organized military attack, if Roman arms should follow in the wake of Roman traders. As in Gaul, tribal jealousies and rivalries were constant; the elaborate defences of great hill-forts like Maiden Castle, Old Sarum, and Hambledon Hill tell their own story of the inter-tribal warfare of those days.

(II) THE COMING OF THE ROMANS

It has been disputed whether political or economic motives predominated in the decision of the Roman government to annex Britain. Cæsar's wars in northern Gaul had led to the brief campaigns of 55 and 54 B.C., which may have increased his personal prestige, but brought no solid advantage to Rome. The resulting closer acquaintance of Rome and the islanders, however, meant that Britain's material resources were well known and already being partially exploited by private enterprise when Claudius seized a political pretext to attack Cymbeline's successor, the king of the Catuvellauni.

If the underlying motive of the invasion of A.D. 43 was to add to the corn-bearing lands of the empire, it is a tribute to the achievement of the generations of Celtic and pre-Celtic tillers of the soil, and in especial to the effects of the heavy-wheeled plough with iron coulter and broad-bladed ploughshare which the Belgae had brought with them to Britain.

The conquest of Britain by the Romans differed from earlier invasions or immigrations not only in its concentrated and unified attack, but in its angle of approach. Where earlier invaders had penetrated up the rivers of the eastern and southern coasts, and advanced along the lines of the chalk uplands, the Romans, with their base on the Continent, had to work from the south-east, across the geological grain, as it were.

To tackle the more war-like tribes of the north-west after the comparatively rapid conquest of the south-eastern regions they had again and again to descend from the ridges into the marshy lowlands and cross one wooded valley after another. The necessity of establishing and maintaining lines of communication for the Roman legions led inevitably, and at once, to the laying down of the great military roads that radiate from the south-east to all parts of Britain. The inadequacy of Camulodunum (the later Colchester) as a base was evident almost at once, and thus London came into existence as the supply depot of the troops, the key to continental trade, and the centre for a unified control that had never before been known in Britain. Up these roads the armies advanced, establishing temporary camps like Channelbank or Pennymuir, forts like Manchester, Carlisle, or Catterick, legionary headquarters like Chester or York.

In a few years the south-east, and then the south-west, were organized as Roman provinces, though a terrible and tragic attempt was made in Cymbeline's kingdom to regain independence by the rising of A.D. 61 in which the Roman inhabitants of London, Camulodunum, and Verulam were massacred. After some thirty-five years of hard fighting the highlands of Wales had been subdued and the Solway reached; and the effective control of the Romans never went beyond these limits, though for a while the region between the Tyne and the Forth was under Roman military supervision, based on the garrisons of Hadrian's Wall.[1]

After A.D. 184 the Scottish lowlands were finally abandoned, and in the third century there was a period of tranquillity and prosperity. But from A.D. 275 onwards the Saxon pirates were menacing the south-eastern coasts of the island, and a

---

[1]Built in A.D. 123 by Hadrian; refortified in 210 by Severus.

Romano-British fleet had to be organized for their defence, whilst from the middle of the fourth century the Picts of Scotland and the Scots of Northern Ireland were raiding Britain from the north-west, and penetrating as far south as Kent, aided by the military roads. The threatened catastrophe was averted for the time being by the general Theodosius, who later became emperor, but other Roman commanders in Britain were less loyal, and made use of the British garrison, amounting at its largest to some 50,000 regulars and auxiliaries, to support their imperial ambitions. The last of a succession of generals who took their troops overseas with them was Constantine III, who left the island to seek his fortune in 407; after that date Britain was never re-garrisoned and had to provide her own defences against the invaders.

For something like four hundred years, as long as from the accession of Elizabeth I to the present day, Britain was part of the Roman Empire. Numerically the Romans were probably fewer than one in ten of the population,[1] and a large proportion of these were occupied with military or frontier duty.

North-west of a line running from the mouth of the Severn to the Humber, the country was a military province, with no towns that were not fortified; it was occupied by the army, but not colonized. South-east of that line Roman civilization of a material kind flourished. Celtic tribal capitals like Exeter, Dorchester, Cirencester, Winchester, Chichester, Canterbury, and Norwich were made the centres of local administration, and converted to planned Roman towns with market-places, town halls, and amphitheatres. Baths and drainage of a kind unknown again in Britain until the nineteenth century were installed. The Roman could not conceive of a civilized life that was not essentially urban.

As the period of military advance was followed by a period of comparative stability, the Roman country house standing in its own estate became a feature of the British country-side. On the skirts of the Cotswolds and the Chilterns, the

[1] In 1917 the English in India were estimated at about one in 1,560 of the population.

Mendips and the North Downs, in the country round Canterbury and Winchester and Bath, the Roman villas were planted,
and in the latter part of the occupation they seem to have
been preferred to the towns, whether because native taste
was prevailing over Italian habits or because the standard
pitched by the towns as planned was too high economically
to be sustained.

Few of the objects discovered in the remains of these villas
have any great artistic merit. The system of hot and cold baths
may be impressive, but the mosaics that covered the floors, when-
ever they go beyond formal geometrical designs, reveal the unfor-
tunate effect of decadent Roman models upon an art of utterly
different traditions. 'The best that most British craftsmen could
achieve was a droll clumsiness.' Though a few pieces of
sculpture, like the stone boss at Bath, show the native genius
informing the masters' technique, there is nothing from the
four centuries of Roman occupation fit to be set beside the
products of the third and second centuries B.C. None the less,
whether preserved in perishable objects or in the un-Romanized
highland regions, the Celtic tradition survived in sufficient
strength to make a notable contribution at a later date to
Anglo-Saxon art.

Purely rural life went on, so far as can be gathered, much
as before, though scientific draining probably greatly increased
the fertility and habitability of the fen country. In the villages
pre-Roman methods of agriculture continued unchanged, but
in the home farms of the villas, which were independent
economic units, the heavier type of plough was consistently used,
and the fields consequently had the long furrows that its use
compelled, as distinct from the small square fields of the old
scratch cultivation.

The many cults and amalgams of Roman with native
religions that the cosmopolitan army of occupation fostered
in Britain had no lasting influence, but Christianity took root
among the British, and when the legionaries left the Church
remained. British bishops attended a church council in Gaul
in the fourth century, and British congregations welcomed the
visit of a Gallican bishop in the fifth century. But it was not

from the British that the Anglo-Saxons were to learn the faith.

Thus the permanent results of the Roman occupation in English history were indirect, and material rather than spiritual. The pattern imposed on English life by the Roman road system has had continuous and lasting influence on the movement both of the inhabitants and the invaders of the country, and even the railway system has not obliterated its importance. So to the natural geography of position and coastline and watercourses and contours must be added the selective activities of the road makers. They have had a lasting effect on our communications, and so on our trade and on the processes of unification and centralization. The natural centre, whether for government or for exchange, is where the lines of communication meet, and in especial where the landway and the waterway meet, as the road crosses the river. The Romans built the first London Bridge; they created London, destined, inevitably, to become the capital of our country.

CHAPTER II

THE PROCESS OF UNIFICATION: THE BRETWEALDAS

(I) INVASION AND SETTLEMENT
(450–600)

HISTORIANS used to tell us that the Britons, left to themselves, were an enervated and effeminate race, unfit to bear arms and incapable of defending themselves. On the contrary, the evidence goes to show that they put up a very good fight against the invaders. But mere courage was not enough; only a strong centralized government could have tackled successfully the problem of organizing the defence of this highly vulnerable island against the simultaneous invaders from so many quarters by so many entrances.

While the Celtic raiders attacked from the north and west, the Humber, the Wash, the lesser creeks of the east coast, the Thames estuary and the harbours all along the south coast from Dover to Southampton Water were penetrated by the long boats of the Angles, the Saxons, and the Jutes. The story written down by the invaders' descendants centuries later, eked out by the fragmentary chronicles of the defenders, has in the last thirty years been rewritten in the light of the patient work of archæologists and philologists.

Objects discovered in graves enable us to locate the pre-Christian settlements; the more or less primitive forms of place-names make it possible to group them in rough chronological order. When this evidence is supplemented by a few extraneous references by continental chroniclers, a picture can be reconstructed of an initial phase somewhere about A.D. 450 when Jutish warriors, invited by British princes to assist in the defence of south-east Britain against other invaders, turned against their employers and opened up the way for invasions by their fellow-countrymen which became the colonization and then the conquest of East Kent. Then, it seems, came the period of landings along the south coast, resulting in settlements in what are now West Kent, Sussex, and Hampshire, while other raiders were penetrating the inlets on the north shores of the Thames estuary and settling on the banks of the Stour, the Blackwater, and the Waveney; entering by the Wash and going up the fenland rivers; entering by the Humber and going up the Ouse and the Trent.

At some stage in this process of invasion and infiltration there came a check and a setback for the Anglo-Saxons, a recovery of ground by the British, and a cessation for at least a generation of any significant military activity, whilst some of the settlers actually returned overseas to their country of origin. It is with this reverse that the Arthurian legend is to be associated; the twelve great battles against the heathen with which Tennyson familiarized Victorian schoolrooms represent the rally of the denizens under the lead of a Romano-British general, whether named Arthur or Ambrosius. British tradition would place this some fifty years after the rising of Hengist, the founder of the Jutish kingdom of Kent; and modern scholarship is prepared to accept the tradition as basically correct.

The temporary recovery of ground by the British may have cut off the invaders who had entered by the Wash and pushed along the Icknield Way to the upper Thames from their base. Certainly 'islands' of British, or Welsh, as the new-comers called them, were left among the Anglo-Saxons at a much later date. However that may be, after a lull lasting roughly from A.D. 500 to 550, the advance was renewed. The Severn Valley was reached by the capture of Gloucester, Cirencester, and Bath in 577; henceforth the Welsh of Cornwall and Devon were cut off from those of Wales. To the north the capture of Chester in 613 by the Anglians, who had established themselves in the Vale of York, isolated the Welsh of the Lake District and Galloway from their southern kindred. Border warfare between the Welsh and the English was to continue on and off for centuries, but the ground secured by the invaders in the century and a half since the settlement began was theirs for good. The larger part of the island had passed into the hands of Teutonic rulers; Britain was to be England.

There is ample evidence of the savagery of the fighting by which the conquest was accomplished, especially in its earlier stages; a savagery which left a long legacy of hatred between the two races. The sixth-century Welsh writer, Gildas, describes the destruction and the massacres in the towns, the flight of the survivors to the hills, or overseas to make a new home for themselves in Brittany, the enslavement of those who surrendered.

But English colonization most certainly did not depend on the exploitation of slaves. The scarcity of British village names is evidence of the extent to which the new-comers made the country their own by mixing their labour with it. The little groups of settlers who founded the Rodings and Dengies and Ingatestones of Essex, the Steynings and Patchings and Cockings of Sussex, made their clearings in the woods, laid out their fields, and tilled their soil by common efforts. In their communal organization of cultivation we see the first signs of those habits of co-operation and common consent which were to be the school for self-government on a larger stage. Nor should their material achievement be forgotten. In the five centuries between Hengist and Edgar the pattern of the English villages as William the Conqueror found them was laid down, and most of the English villages of to-day are to be found in William's great survey.

Now and then, as in the laws of Ine of Wessex, we get a picture of the settlers on land newly conquered from the British—the colonist abandoning his new holding to his lord, or the community of small freemen fencing their fields lest the cows from the common pasture get into the corn—but for the most part the long epic of the plough, 'the hoar enemy of the woodland,' as the Anglo-Saxon riddle calls it, goes untold.

But it is not only to the Anglo-Saxon communities of peasants that we have a debt to acknowledge. The destructive impact of the warbands on a more sophisticated civilization must not be allowed to obscure the fact that they also had a positive and permanent contribution to make, at this early stage, to our social and political traditions. The mutual loyalty of the leader and his war-following, first described by Tacitus in his account of the Germans before they invaded the Roman Empire, may seem a primitive and barbarous substitute for the discipline that informed the Roman state, and of less human value than the ties of kinship that held the Celtic clan together; but it was to be the moral foundation of the social code of England for ages to come.

The faith that binds lord and man, so sacred that to Alfred the Great the breach of it is the only offence irredeemable at law, involving a relationship honourable to both parties and making up the happiness and dignity of life, is reflected in Anglo-Saxon poetry and sermons, in incident after incident of Anglo-Saxon history, from Bede's story of the thegn Lilla, who took the dagger of the assassin in his lord's place, to the poet's account of the thegns of the ealdorman Byrhtnoth at the battle of Maldon, seventy-five years before the Norman Conquest, carrying on to the death a fight that they knew to be hopeless rather than leave their lord's death unavenged.

On this tie of lordship and loyalty could be based the early federations that made possible a combined effort against the Britons, and the honourable relationship between king and overking that prepared the way for the later unification of England; on it could be based the delegation of responsibility by a monarchy that had not as yet evolved a nation-wide machinery of administration; from it could develop the wider loyalty of subject and king, and the responsibility of ruler and master for the welfare of subject and servant; and from the acceptance of the sanctity of plighted faith in one special relationship there could develop the sense of the sanctity of a man's word, to whomsoever it was given.

As the country was mastered, lands were assigned to the war companions of the leaders, and the leaders themselves became kings, endowed with royal estates and with rights to tribute and to entertainment on the lands of others. There must have been varying numbers of small dominions in the sixth century, and that the Anglo-Saxon princes fought against each other as well as the Welsh is attested by the ancient fortifications, such as the series of dykes that cut across the Icknield Way in Cambridgeshire, in the ditches of which piled skeletons have been found, and by the traces of other defensive works which indicate the clash of Middle Anglian and East Saxon at the point where the Roman Road from Colchester to Godmanchester crossed the Cam under the little ruined Roman camp on whose site William the Conqueror was later to plant Cambridge Castle.)

But the details of these 'wars of kites and crows,' as Milton called them, are utterly obscure, and it is not until the Roman missionaries bring letters to England, at the beginning of the seventh century, that the mists begin to clear away from the face of the land, and with the help of our first great English historian, Bede, we can make out a rough map of the England in which his saints and heroes were to work.

(II) BEDE AND HIS ENGLAND
(600–735)

We begin with Bede's own country of Northumbria, founded by Anglians, stretching from the Humber to the Forth, and divided by the Tees into two kingdoms that merged and separated by turns for centuries as local or dynastic feelings moved them. Then, immediately south of the Humber, came the kingdom of Lindsey, centred on Lincoln. Next, beyond the Wash, were the kingdoms of East Anglia (Norfolk and Suffolk), and of the East Saxons (Essex, Middlesex, and part of Surrey), with London as its chief town. South of the Thames came the kingdoms of Kent, of the South Saxons (Sussex), and of the West Saxons, stretching from the Thames Valley to the Channel. North of the Thames and south of the Humber the central block of the midlands was ruled in Bede's day by the kings of Mercia, the kingdom that took its name from the marches or borderland that separated the upper waters of the Trent with its Anglian settlements from the upper waters of the Severn, still occupied by the Welsh. From a centre near Birmingham the Mercian power spread eastwards and southwards, swallowing up many lesser groups of settlers, from the mouth of the Severn to the fenlands, and absorbing the kingdom of the Middle Angles, the neighbours and rivals of the East Anglians.

The possibilities opened up by the intersection of two main Roman highways in the middle of England, the Fosse Way running from Exeter to Lincoln, and the Watling Street running from London to Chester, may help to account both for the military achievements of the Mercian kings, and for that commercial activity which is permanently registered for Englishmen in the word *penny*, which may have got its name from Penda, the villain of Bede's story, who died as the last pagan king of Mercia in the year 655.

The battles which punctuate Bede's narrative arise from three different types of conflict. There may be the rivalry of two kinsmen of the blood royal for the rule over one kingdom; there may be the standing struggle of the English with their natural opponents the British or the Scots; and there may be the competition between two Anglo-Saxon kingdoms for ascendancy or hegemony over the others.

What this ascendancy meant in practice in a thinly peopled country with few, if any, fixed frontiers, with different racial traditions and customs, and at varying levels of culture, some pagan, and some Christian, can only be roughly indicated; but it probably carried with it the right to name or displace the lesser kings, the establishment of personal ties of mutual loyalty between them and the overking, and an obligation on their part to pay tribute on some roughly calculated scale of households or families.

To these overkings the West Saxon chronicler of the ninth century was to give the name of Bretwealda, the English version of the title *Rex Britanniæ*—Ruler of Britain—which Bede gives to seven Anglo-Saxon kings who, he says, were lords of all England south of the Humber, and who may be fairly regarded as the forerunners in the slow process of the unification of England.

The first two Bretwealdas, Aelle of the South Saxons (about 477-491) and Ceawlin of the West Saxons (about 560-584), were leaders in the struggle of the first century and a half between the English and the Britons, and little is known of them. The third, Ethelbert of Kent (584–616), ruled a kingdom whose Jutish culture indicates closer contacts with the Continent than Angles or Saxons had preserved.

Ethelbert's Christian wife and the ceremonial of his court came from Gaul, and he was the first of English kings to accept the Christian faith, the first to set down the laws of his land in writing, and the first of Teutonic rulers to do so in the vernacular. Bede has less to say of his fourth Bretwealda, Raedwald of East Anglia. The marvellous treasure store unearthed at Sutton Hoo, not five miles from his palace, though it must be assigned to a rather later period, is the best comment on the splendour of an East Anglian king in this age.

With Edwin of Northumbria, fifth on the list, who accepted Christianity for himself and his people in the year 627, the period of the Northumbrian ascendancy begins, continued under Oswald (633–641) and Oswiu (654–657); an ascendancy based on successful warfare against Britons, Picts, and Scots, and acknowledged by them, as well as by the English kingdoms south of the Humber: an ascendancy characterized by a culture that is the fruit of both Celtic and Roman Christianity, and by a society of saints and scholars, of monasteries and dioceses ruled by nobles and members of the royal family. Of this culture Bede is himself the fine flower.

As far as posterity is concerned, Bede is the first articulate Englishman. In his greatest and best-known work, the *Ecclesiastical History of the English People*, he briefly describes his own quiet life, spent from the age of seven in the monastery of Wearmouth-Jarrow in the pursuit of godliness and good learning; 'observing monastic discipline and the daily care of singing in the church, and always delighting in learning, teaching, and writing.'

That a pioneer historian with no models to guide him should also be one of the greatest of English historians is amazing. His greatness lies not only in the scope of his conception—the history of the English people as one race, though ruled by many kings and princelings; the history of the English people as a Christian community, forming part of the Church universal; the history of the English people as a stage in world history, following on the world empire of Rome 'crushed by the Goths in the year 409.'[1] To this breadth of vision and the resultant power of structure in composition Bede adds a historical conscience of the first quality.

There were many gaps in his knowledge; he was as far from the coming of Hengist as we are to-day from the restoration of Charles II, the conversion of Kent by the Roman missionaries was as remote from him as Trafalgar is from us, and for the early centuries written evidence was almost totally lacking, but he is never tempted to fill in the gaps with romantic inventions like those of Geoffrey of Monmouth or Lytton Strachey.

He collects his facts from all available sources, written and oral; he gives the names of those who supplied him with information; he distinguishes between the eye-witness's narrative (which he often reproduces verbatim), the written document (which he quotes in full), the tradition handed down, and the tale passed from mouth to mouth. He gives references to his written authorities, and specifically begs the copyists not to leave them out—an injunction which they disobeyed.

The frequency with which he records what he regards as miraculous events does not stamp him as uncritical. What Bernard Shaw's fifteenth-century bishop says of St. Joan holds good even more emphatically of seventh-century England; a miracle is an event which confirms faith, and if amid the greater marvels of the extension of Christendom we read of lesser marvels of healing, of second sight, or of docile birds and beasts, these do not warrant us in doubting the carefulness and truth of Bede's history. And lastly, Bede's sense of chronology stamps him as the genuine historian.

It was he who established the Christian era as our method of reckoning of historical time. The earliest documents that he quotes, the letters of Pope Gregory to the missionary Augustine of Canterbury, are dated by 'the fourteenth year of the Emperor

[1] By modern reckoning, the year 410.

Maurice and the fourteenth indiction.' The decrees of the synod of Heathfield, held by Archbishop Theodore, are dated by 'the tenth year of Egfrith of Northumbria, the sixth year of Ethelfrid of Mercia, the seventeenth year of Aldulf of East Anglia, and the seventh year of Hlothere of Kent'; but Bede himself dated the council 'in the year from the incarnation of our Lord 680.' He ends his history with a brief chronological summary of the leading events of his narrative, from Julius Cæsar's invasion '60 B.C.' down to the year in which he is writing, 'A.D. 731'; a chapter that most modern readers would skip as a dry recapitulation, but which imports not only a startling innovation, of incalculable practical value to writers, readers, and administrators, but a philosophy of history; a recognition of the heavenly harmony and order imposed on the chaotic unknown of past and future by the central mystery of the Christian faith.

In the early days of English Christianity there were frequent relapses to paganism. The correspondence between Gregory the Great and Augustine of Canterbury raises many of the problems familiar to missionaries to-day in relation to the risks of too sudden a break with the social traditions of pre-Christian days, and a syncretic cult may have been attempted by others besides Raedwald of East Anglia who 'had in the same temple an altar to sacrifice to Christ, and another small one to offer victims to devils.'

In Northumbria a further problem was raised, also, unfortunately, familiar in the modern mission field, of divergence in ritual between the missionaries who came from Iona with Aidan, after a pagan reaction had driven the Roman missionaries out in 633, and the returned Romanists. The Northumbrian decision for Rome had been taken at Whitby ten years before Bede's birth, but he still attached to the controversy on the date of Easter an importance that puzzles his modern readers.

This does not prevent him from recognizing wholeheartedly the English Church's debt to men like Aidan or Chad, or depicting with loving care their pastoral work and their saintly lives. The religion and learning in which he was bred was the

legacy of Iona as well as of Rome, and by Bede's time the
fusion with the native heritage was complete. Bede wrote English
poems as well as Latin prose, and his *Ecclesiastical History*
is the work of an Englishman proud of his people, whose love
of God and man can express itself freely and naturally in either
tongue.

Thus the native freshness of his story-telling has added to
our literary tradition a whole series of pictures familiar to
hundreds who have no notion of their origin—the Anglian
slave boys in the Roman market-place; the feasters in the
fire-lit hall through which the frightened sparrow flies, from
darkness to darkness; the pale, hook-nosed, dark-eyed Paulinus
baptizing converts in the River Trent; and the symbolic figure
of the monastery servant, Caedmon, reciting to the Abbess
Hilda the poem he had dreamed in the stable, the first English
hymn, marking the annexation by Christian art of the heroic
traditions of pagan Anglo-Saxon verse.

Bede in himself makes clear to us the warming, enriching,
integrating effects of the Christian religion upon the bewildered
and scattered minds of the peoples of seventh-century England.

In his final chapter the old scholar, for so he sees himself
at the age of sixty-two, sets down alongside his vertical line
of time a horizontal survey of England at the time when he is
writing. Mercia, once the great pagan obstacle in the path of
evangelization, is the home of the newly consecrated Archbishop of Canterbury, Tatwine; the bishops of the other Sees
of Kent, Essex, East Anglia, Wessex, Mercia, the western
marches, and Sussex are enumerated, and 'all these provinces
and their kings are subject to King Aethelbald of Mercia,'
though Bede does not accord that ruler the title that he himself
claimed of Ruler of Britain.

The Picts are at peace with the English, and the disputes
that divided the Churches of the two races are ended, though
the British are still schismatics. In Bede's own Northumbria,
Wilfrid is Archbishop of York, and Ceolwulf, to whom the
history is dedicated, is king. 'The times are so peaceable and
calm that many of the Northumbrians are laying aside their
weapons and inclining to the tonsure and monastic vows, both

for themselves and for their children, rather than to the study
of martial discipline; what will be the end hereof the next age
will show.'

(III) THE MERCIAN SUPREMACY
(670–796)

The days of the Northumbrian ascendancy were, in fact,
over before Bede's death. The line of kings who had exercised
overlordship south of the Humber, and at times over British,
Picts, and Scots also, had ended when Oswiu died in 670, and
the supremacy had passed to Mercia.

Neither Bede nor the later West Saxon chronicler were
willing to recognize the great Mercian kings who dominated
England from the middle of the seventh to the end of the
eighth century as worthy of the title of Bretwealda. Bede's
theme of the expansion of Christianity naturally led him to
deny the honour to Mercia, the pagan nation whose pagan
king had slain two Christian kings of Northumbria (Edwin
and Oswald), whilst the rivalry of Wessex and Mercia for the
possession of the upper Thames valley and the overlordship
of Kent, accounts for the West Saxon refusal to recognize the
notable contribution of Wulfhere (665–674), Aethelbald (716–
757), and Offa (757–796) to the unification of England.

This, together with the fact that it was the West Saxon
kings who ultimately made England one kingdom, whilst
Danish occupation obliterated the older landmarks of the
midlands, explains the injustice that has been done in the past
to these great rulers. Even Stubbs speaks of 'the evil days of
Mercian supremacy.' Offa's laws, of which Alfred the Great
spoke with respect, are lost, and there is no eighth-century
Mercian literature to set beside the achievements of seventh-
century Northumbria or tenth-century Wessex, but charters,
canons, and coins survive, and from them modern scholars
have succeeded in piecing together the picture of the rise and
dominance of Mercia.

It is the story of the amalgamation of the central regions of
England by rulers who added to their earliest lands round
Tamworth the groups of settlers who made up the Middle

Anglian region, the kingdom of Lindsey, the country of the Hwicce in the Severn valley, and the district now known as Oxfordshire and Berkshire; made and unmade the kings of Essex, Kent, and Wessex, established for a short time (788–796) a metropolitan see in the midlands, and summoned to their councils the leading churchman of every diocese south of the Humber. The pagan reputation of Penda is cast into the shade by Offa, the founder of St. Albans Abbey and of the arch-bishopric of Lichfield.

Significant evidence of the far-ranging administrative activities of the Mercian overlords is supplied by the ancient document called *The Tribal Hidage*, which is assigned by the best authorities to the days of the Mercian ascendancy. It enumerates a number of districts or regions in terms of the number of households or families they contain—undoubtedly for the practical purpose of guiding the ruler's servants who are to levy the tribute payable to him. It indicates a central organization and a standardization of contributions over a wide area—ranging from the settlers by the Peak to those by the Wrekin and Chilterns, from the dwellers in Lindsey and Elmet to those near Hitchin and Wychwood, and covering the peoples of Kent, Sussex, East Anglia, Essex, and Wessex, and it thus resumes in itself the process by which the numerous primitive settlements of the Midlands had been welded together by the rulers who, in the seventh and eighth centuries, could exact tribute from all the kings south of the Humber.

Geographically, Tamworth made an admirable base for expansion. It stood at the head of the great waterway of the Trent, leading to Lindsey and the Vale of York; and between the points at which the Ryknield Street that runs from Evesham to Doncaster, and the Fosse Way that runs from Bath to Lincoln, crossed the Watling Street that ran from Chester to London. Not the least significant feature of the Mercian suprem-acy is the fact that under Aethelbald and Offa, London had been detached from Essex and had become a Mercian town. It is this command of communications that helps to explain the commercial character of the Mercian supremacy, and it is their commerce that accounts for their widespread relations. The penny first coined by Mercian kings was used as the scale of calculating legal penalties in eighth-century Wessex, and it circulated in Merovingian Gaul.

The golden coins of Offa give evidence of contacts with the caliphate. The earliest commercial treaty to be negotiated between an English king and a foreign ruler is to be found in the correspondence between Offa and Charlemagne, which established the legal status of the merchants of either party in the lands of the other, and which contains the first reference to the English textile industry and its regulation by government.

'Pilgrims who are making their way to Rome,' writes Charles to his dearest brother, Offa, king of the Mercians, 'shall pass peacefully and unmolested through our lands. We have found, however, that some of them dishonestly dabble in trade, pursuing profit, not religion, and if we find any such, they will be made to pay the usual tolls. You wrote to us about merchants; we extend to them our personal protection, as is the old custom for those engaged in trade. If they are treated wrongfully, let them appeal to us or to our judges, and we will see that they have full justice. Similarly, if any of our subjects suffer injustice in your realm, they shall appeal to you for a just remedy, so that no trouble may come about between our subjects. We have sent you the black stones that your excellency was anxious to have; our agent has orders to find out what kind you want, to procure them for you, and make arrangements for transport. Just as you informed us of your wishes as to the length of the stones, our subjects are demanding that you will give orders that the cloths from your country shall be of the same length as those you used to send us.'

The lasting monument of Offa's power is the great earthwork that bears his name. Mercia, it will be remembered, took its name from the March lands, and Offa's Dyke, which runs from the Irish Sea to the Bristol Channel, marks the frontier between his kingdom and the lands of the Welsh. It corresponds pretty closely to the natural line that divides the ancient rocks of the Welsh mountains from the younger hills of the Severn and Wye valleys, and differs only in detail from the

modern boundary between England and Wales. Whilst following a sound strategical line for defence it was neither a military
barrier nor a racial frontier; it was a boundary defined by
agreement between the Welsh of the hills and the Mercians of
the lowlands. Recent minute investigation indicates that the
work was planned as a whole and executed simultaneously by
locally organized gangs, probably during the later years of
Offa's reign. It has been called the greatest public work of the
Anglo-Saxon period, and testifies as certainly as Offa's
correspondence with Charlemagne to the assured character of
his ascendancy in Britain.

Offa's last years, none the less, were marked by the signs
of the storm that was to break on England and Europe. Legend
tells how Charlemagne wept at the sight of the Viking ships
off the north-western coasts of Frankland, and his Northumbrian friend and teacher, Alcuin, the pupil of Bede's pupils,
wrote to commiserate his fellow countrymen on the sacking of
Lindisfarne by the Northmen in 793.

The challenge of the Danish invaders was to meet with a
response which neither the Roman nor the Anglo-Saxon
invaders had evoked, and if we try to answer the question why
Alfred succeeded where Caractacus and Arthur had failed,
we shall have to take into account other considerations besides
the character of the greatest Englishman who has ever reigned
in this island. 'Out of war is born the king,' and the many
internecine wars of the shifting kingdoms of seventh- and
eighth-century England had not obliterated, but rather
strengthened the sense of common blood and common interest
that made possible the shadowy institution of the Bretwealdaship. The attribution of the title to Aelle of Sussex stands for a
tradition of common action, possibly even of a confederation
of the English invaders against the British in the last years of
the fifth century; its second bearer, Ceawlin of Wessex, is
recognized as leader in the renewed advance of the English
which carried them to the shores of the Bristol Channel a
century later; and the overlordship of Kentish, East Anglian,
and Northumbrian kings was acknowledged not only by the
payment of tribute but by marriage alliances.

Time and again Bede tells of such intermarriages between the kingdoms, which assume a sense of common kinship; of Ethelburga of Kent, who brought her chaplain with her when she married the still pagan Edwin of Deira; of the West Saxon wife of Oswald of Northumbria; of the sister and daughter of Penda of Mercia, married to Cenwalch of Wessex and Alfrid of Northumbria; of the sister princesses of East Anglia, married one to a Northumbrian and the other to a Kentish king, who became, in succession, abbesses of Ely.

By the eighth century, as we have seen, this overlordship was no longer shadowy, nor did it represent a merely military ascendancy. The authority of the Mercian kings is registered in treaties, in charters confirming the gifts of land made by lesser kings to houses of religion, in judgments given by councils competent to act for the whole Anglo-Saxon Church. Although Bede had refused to recognize Aethelbald as Bretwealda, he had described the kings of all the provinces south of Humber as subject to him, and Offa, who more often used the style of 'King of the Mercians and the other nations round about,' once, at least, described himself in an official document as 'King of all England'—*Rex totius Anglorum patriæ*. When Offa died in 796, and the title of Bretwealda passed to the West Saxon, Egbert, its attributes were no longer imponderable.

But it was the struggle with the Danish invaders that was to put an end to the Bretwealdaship and create a national kingship. Not even the unction bestowed by the Church on Offa's son, in imitation of the Frankish rite, could sanctify the royal office as did Alfred's fight for Christendom. The English monarchy which Elizabeth inherited descends, in spirit as in blood, from Alfred, king of the West Saxons.

CHAPTER III

THE PROCESS OF UNIFICATION: THE WEST SAXON RESPONSE TO THE DANISH CHALLENGE

(1) THE RISE OF WESSEX
(577–839)

THE West Saxon monarchy which was to furnish the last of the Bretwealdas and the first of the national kings, and ultimately to extend its system of government, if not of law, to all England, was founded, according to its own tradition, by Cerdic, who landed in Southampton Water in 495. The permanent settlers in that region, however, seem to have been Jutes, probably the allies of the Saxons, who themselves made their way inland, penetrating to the middle Thames valley.

There, it would seem, they met other Saxons who had entered by the Wash and made their way up the Ouse and along the Icknield Way, which crosses the Thames some ten miles south-east of Dorchester, where the first West Saxon bishopric was to be planted in 635, and runs along the Downs above Wantage, the birthplace of Alfred. The British recovery of ground in the early sixth century probably cut the contacts between the Thames and Ouse valleys for the time being, and when West Saxon advance was renewed in the sixth century, the movement towards the north-east was frustrated, while that to the west led to Ceawlin's victory at Dyrham in 577, which took him to the Cotswolds and Mendips.

Mercian pressure from the north made south-western expansion the obvious course; the Severn valley was abandoned as well as the region round Dorchester-on-Thames, and the West Saxons overran the regions now known as Somerset, Dorset, and Devon. By the end of the seventh century they had taken Exeter, and the remarkable absence of Celtic place-names in Devonshire to-day indicates a most thorough colonization.

The issuing of the first body of West Saxon laws about 694 by Ine of Wessex may have been due in part to the need to define the legal status of the 'Welsh' left in the newly settled lands, and the rights and duties of the Saxon settlers, but it indicates also a conception of the relations of kingship and law which was to be of immeasurable importance in the future history of England. The extension of West Saxon power to the east begins under Ine; he was able to impose his commands on the rulers of Kent and Sussex, and his control of Surrey, the 'southern region' of the East Saxon kingdom, is indicated by his description of the Bishop of London as 'my bishop.'

All through the eighth century, however, the power of Mercia made a West Saxon hegemony impossible. Not till the death of Berhtric, Offa's son-in-law, imposed by him as king on the West Saxons, did the subordination of Wessex to Mercia end with the return of Egbert from exile overseas in 802, and not till Egbert had been king for twenty years was it possible for him to be regarded as Bretwealda. In 825 he defeated the ruler of Mercia at Ellandun, and Kent, Essex, Surrey, and Sussex became subject to him. Four years later he conquered Mercia, where Offa's line had come to an end, and was recognized as overlord by the Northumbrians. Though his effective supremacy over the Midlands was short-lived, he had united all England south of the Thames for good, and had thus made possible his grandson's resistance to the Danish invaders.

His personal legacy was at least as precious. The descendants of Egbert were a good stock; for six generations vigorous, upright, prolific, and loyal to each other. One of the poems in the Anglo-Saxon collection called the *Exeter Book* speaks of the wretchedness of the man who has no kindred. 'Better were it for him that he had a brother, and they both the sons of one man, if he should attack a boar or subdue a bear, that beast with cruel paws. Ever should those men take counsel and sleep together; they should never be divided by dissension till death part them.'

Confronted by cruel and treacherous invaders, honouring neither God nor their pledged word, nothing but faith in their fellows can save men from the paralysis of despair. It was in the strong trust that the West Saxon princes showed and roused that the strength of the West Saxon resistance to the invaders lay. We recognize it in the loyalty of Alfred's thegns and ealdormen to their lord, in the strong tie between Alfred and his brothers, in the long fighting partnership of Alfred's son and daughter, in the comradeship in arms of his two grandsons at Brunanburh. 'God created natural friends in kinsmen,' said Alfred himself.

(II) THE DANISH INVASIONS AND ALFRED THE GREAT
(835–899)

The wave of Viking invasion which struck England in the ninth century was part of a great movement, the outermost ripples of which reached to Moscow, Byzantium, and Greenland. As far as England and France were concerned, its violence is partly attributable to the extension of Carolingian dominion, which eliminated the rival sea power of the Frisians. 'The landing of the heathen men in Sheppey' in 835, four years before Egbert's death, opened a series of raids along the eastern and southern coasts of England, in Lindsey, East Anglia, Kent, Hampshire, and Somerset, which taught men the meaning of the fury of the Northmen. In 865, when Egbert's third grandson had just become king of the West Saxons, the character of the attacks changed to a concerted plan of invasion. A large army aiming at conquest and settlement landed in England. In the next eight years, they succeeded in establishing a subject kingdom centred on York, defeated and killed Edmund, the king of East Anglia, who refused to purchase his life by apostasy, occupied London, and set up a subject ruler in Mercia. A systematic colonization of Yorkshire by Danish settlers was carried through in 876, and, in 877, a district corresponding to the later shires of Lincoln, Leicester, Derby, and Nottingham was likewise settled by Danish warriors, the western part of Mercia being left to the rule of an English king subject to Danish authority.

Wessex had not been left in peace during those years; in 870 a Danish army based on Reading made savage attacks on the surrounding country, and Aethelred the king, with his brother Alfred, who succeeded him in 871, fought a series of obstinate but inconclusive actions, leading to a purchased peace in 872. In 875 another Danish army descended on Dorset, moving thence to Devon in 876, and then on to Gloucestershire in 877, outwitting the West Saxons by violation of treaty agreements and by surprise marches.

Early in 878 they occupied Chippenham and it looked as if the last independent English kingdom was to fall. All Wessex east of Selwood, the dense forest that then lay to the west of Salisbury Plain, submitted to the Danes; the resistants either fled overseas or followed King Alfred into the marsh country of Somerset.

There was a royal estate at Athelney, on Sedgemoor, and from that base Alfred harried the Danes all through the spring of 878 and at last, successfully rallying the forces of the shires of Somerset, Wiltshire, and Hampshire, defeated the Danish army at Edington on the northern slopes of Salisbury Plain. Its leader, Guthrum, accepted baptism, and finally abandoned the attempt to subject Wessex to Danish rule. Instead he moved to East Anglia, and established there the third Danish colony on English soil.

Edington was by no means Alfred's last battle. In 884 he had to defend the shores of the Thames estuary both by land and at sea against fresh Viking attacks. Two years later he took London, which had been in Danish control since 872. The acquisition was of the greatest strategic and political importance; it marked out Alfred as the leader of national resistance.

'All the English people who were not under the Danes submitted to Alfred,' says the chronicler, and his godson Guthrum, now king of Danish East Anglia, entered into a treaty with him which made the Watling Street, the Ouse, the Lee, and the Thames the frontier line between the lands under

English and Danish law, and defined the legal status of the racial minorities on either side of the border. English Mercia, including London, had its own governor, the ealdorman Aethelred, who recognized Alfred as his lord, and was given to wife Alfred's daughter, Aethelflaed, the famous Lady of Mercia.)

But still more Danes came from overseas, and the Danes of Northumbria made common cause with them. The Anglo-Saxon chronicle, for whose compilation Alfred himself was responsible, tells in detail the story of the struggle from 892 to 896, waged in Kent, Surrey, and Sussex, and of the measures taken by Alfred; the building of warships 'twice as large as those of the Danes'; the construction of a system of fortress towns for the defence of the southern shires, guarded by permanent garrisons drawn from the surrounding country, and the distribution of the available manpower between military and agricultural duty so as to make long campaigns practicable.)

When Alfred died in 899 he had saved England from subjection to heathenism, and made sure that it would be ruled by West Saxon kings. He had acquired in London an invaluable base for the reconquest of the Danelaw; he had laid down the lines on which successful warfare was to be waged; and he had left a valiant pair trained by himself to carry on the task, his son Edward, as king of the West Saxons, and his daughter Aethelflaed, the Lady of Mercia.

But England's debt to Alfred does not end with his military achievements. He was a victor whose uses for peace went beyond preparation for the next war, and he was a man of action who had a just value for study. He had a deep sense of the dignities of kingship, but his interpretation of its duties sets him apart. For he held that progress was bound up with Christian knowledge, and that this knowledge was not a mystery to be reserved for priests and monks, but a treasure to be shared by laymen. Bede had loved to instruct his convent pupils; Alfred believed that education should be for public life. The young nobles who fought at his side, the ealdormen and reeves who presided over the popular assemblies where justice was done, the men that held the forts, the masters who commanded the ships, all needed the wisdom that had come down from the past to direct their courses well. ('Men of action could not find the time available to monks and choristers to learn Latin, but they could be taught to read their mother tongue, and it was the king's concern to see that there were books for them to read.')

Two generations of the Northmen's raids had broken up the ancient nurseries of learning, and Alfred himself draws a piteous, possibly over-coloured, picture of the decay of letters since the great days of English scholarship. He fetched scholars from Germany, from France, from Wales, and from Mercia to Wessex and became their pupil, gradually acquiring, in the lull between the wars, enough Latin to become himself our first great translator. 'When I remembered how the knowledge of Latin had decayed, and yet many could read English writing, I began, among other various and manifold troubles of a kingdom, to translate into English this book, sometimes word by word, and sometimes according to the sense.'

Bede wrote for clerks, Alfred for the young men who knew their native legends, but were ignorant of the great European literary tradition. 'Where are now the bones of Wayland, the famous goldsmith?' is his rendering of Boethius' *'Ubi nunc fidelis ossa Fabricii manent?'* And if his biographer, Asser, may be believed, he expected his officials to use the opportunities provided.

'I wonder at your assurance,' he would say, 'that, having taken upon yourselves, by God's favour and mine, the rank and office of wise men, you have neglected the studies of the wise. Either abandon at once the exercise of the temporal powers that you possess, or endeavour more zealously to study the lessons of wisdom.' 'And so, wonderful to relate,' says Asser, 'almost all his ealdormen and officials, though unlearned from childhood, gave themselves up to the study of letters, preferring an unfamiliar discipline to the loss of office.'

Alfred saw knowledge as strictly relevant to the life of action, but he had also that pure passion for knowledge for its own sake that must be the driving force in any literary renaissance. Heaven is for him the place where all riddles are answered. 'That man is very foolish and very wretched who will not increase his intelligence while he is in this world, and also desire to come to the eternal life where nothing is hid from him.'

He can elaborate Pope Gregory the Great's advice to the teacher to adapt his methods to the varying capacities of his pupils—'As the harper variously draws and touches the stretched strings of a harp, touching them all with the same hand, though he touches them differently'; but he has also in full measure the teacher's desire not only to instruct, but to stimulate pupils to seek for themselves. In the metrical epilogue to his translation of Gregory's *Pastoral Care* he calls on all his readers to 'bring their pitchers for themselves and draw for their drinking from the living waters, deep and still.'

Most moving of all is his preface to his last book, that in which, as Asser says, he collected flowers from many fields. Alfred sees himself rather as a woodcutter than as a stroller down flowery paths.

'I then gathered for myself staves, and stud-shafts, and cross-beams, and helves for each of the tools that I could work with; and bow-timbers and bolt-timbers for every work that I could perform—as many as I could carry of the comeliest trees. Nor came I home with a burden, for it pleased me not to bring all the wood home, even if I could bear it. In each tree I saw something that I needed at home; therefore I exhort everyone who is able, and has many wains, to direct his steps to the selfsame wood where I cut the stud-shafts. Let him there obtain more for himself, and load his wains with fair twigs, so that he may wind many a neat wall and erect many a rare house, and build a fair enclosure, and therein dwell in joy and comfort both winter and summer, in such manner as I have not yet done. But He who taught me, and to whom the wood was pleasing, hath power to make me dwell more comfortably, both in this transitory cottage by the road, while I am on this world-pilgrimage, and also in the everlasting home which He hath promised us.'

The man who reveals himself to us in these writings is a Christian, a student, and an artist, sensitive not only to fine craftsmanship and to the music of strings and words, but to the beauty of the world of nature about him. He is translating the Soliloquies of the recently converted Augustine. 'Seasons return on themselves, stars set and rise again,' says Augustine. 'Yes,' says Alfred, 'but all come not again where they formerly were, nor become just what they were, but others come in their stead, as leaves on trees, and apples, grass, plants, and trees grow old and sere and others come, wax green and grow and ripen and begin to wither . . . yea, even men's bodies wax old. But as they formerly lived more worthily than trees and animals, so shall they arise more worthily in Doomsday.'

The trees of an English landscape—'the fairest thing in God's creation'—replace the evergreen foliage of the Mediterranean, and in place of the brilliant young scholar hardly yet weaned from Neoplatonism, to whom Change is a great abstraction, we see the man who knows his work is nearly done, and is ready to fall like the ripe apple from the tree; but the grass will be green next year and for him there is the resurrection.

England has known other kings who were good artists and devout Christians—Henry III, Richard II, Henry VI, Charles I—but only Alfred was both a good artist and a good ruler. In the preface to his laws we hear the same voice; it reveals his dignity, modesty, practical commonsense, and the sense that all good work is done for God.

'I, King Alfred, gathered these laws together, and commanded many which our forefathers held and which seemed good to me, to be written down, and many of those which did not seem good to me I rejected upon the advice of my wise men. I dared not set down in writing much of my own, for I knew not how much of it would please those who should come after us. But what I found—of the days of Ine, my kinsman, or of Offa, King of the Mercians, or of Aethelbert, who was the first of the English race to receive baptism— which seemed most just to me, those I have gathered here, and rejected the others. I, then, Alfred, King of the West

Saxons, showed all these unto my wise men, and they said that it seemed good unto them all that they should be kept.'

The observations on the duties of kings, which Alfred added as he translated the history of Orosius, illuminate Asser's picture of the king concerned for the good learning of his young nobles, seeing that justice was done in the folk moots, keeping the easy-going West Saxons up to the mark in building fortifications. 'The authority and power which the ruler receives for the benefit of many he must exhibit outwardly, but keep his humility inwardly.' 'The proud and unrighteous king, seated on high, girt about with thegns decked with golden helmets, is no better than one of his own servants if he be stripped of his raiment and his following.'

The scholar had sought to hand on the torch to those who should come after; in one of his additions to his translation of Boethius, Alfred tells what the king has tried to do.

'I did not long for this earthly authority, but I desired tools and material for the work which I was bidden to do; that was, virtuously and fittingly to wield and exercise the power which was entrusted to me. . . . The material of the king, and the tools with which to rule, are a well-peopled land; he ought to have men for prayer, men for war, and men for labour. . . . This also is his material—to have, in addition to these tools, provision for these three classes; land to dwell in, and gifts and weapons and meat and ale and raiment.

'Without these he can not keep his tools in order, nor without his tools do any of those things which he is bidden to do. . . . Now to speak most briefly, this it is that I have desired—to live worthily while I lived, and, after my life, to leave to the men who should follow me, my memory in good deeds.'

This voice from the ninth century evokes even to-day some of the affection that we recognize in the chronicler's phrase relating the meeting of Alfred with his troops before Edington, 'They were fain of his presence'; and in Alfred's medieval byname, 'England's herdman, England's darling.' The friendly legend of the cakes may or may not be true, but ever since its first telling it has served to keep alive popular awareness of the king whose heroism was equalled by his sanity and simplicity, and whose determination that learning should be a uniting and not a dividing force, available for those who fought and laboured as well as for those who prayed, has helped to make the English tongue what it is.

(iii) The Reconquest of the Danelaw
(886–955)

Alfred died in the last year of the ninth century, and his children and grandchildren carried on his work. Edward and his sister, working along his lines, built up a system of fortified villages and towns in key positions in the Midlands, some, like Towcester on the Watling Street, on Roman sites; some, like Wallingford and Oxford, newly planned.

From 909 onwards they took the offensive, and by a series of battles secured the submission of the eastern Midlands. In the thirty years that the Danes had ruled there, Christianity had spread amongst them; Englishmen had freely acquired and exploited land, inter-marriage had taken place. There was no sudden or revolutionary change for the dwellers in Essex, East Anglia, and the districts dependent on Cambridge, Bedford, Northampton, Derby, Leicester, Stamford, and Lincoln when the armies belonging to those towns submitted to Edward or Aethelflaed.

By the end of 918 all the Danes south of the Humber had accepted English rule, and the death of Aethelflaed and her husband had led to the final fusion of Mercia and Wessex as one kingdom under Edward, whilst the Welsh princes, now his immediate neighbours, recognized him as their overlord. The Danes who belonged to York had before this approached Aethelflaed for assistance against the attacks of the Norse Vikings, who had been invading Cumberland and Galloway from their colonies in Ireland, and who took York in 920.

Edward made no attempt to oust them, but after his death his son, Athelstan, completed the assertion of English supremacy over the Scandinavians by driving out the Norwegian King of York in 927. Ten years later his position was challenged by the allied forces of the Norse ruler of Dublin, the King of the Scots, and the British King of Strathclyde, but they were utterly defeated at Brunanburh, an unidentified site, by Athelstan and his brother Edmund. 'Never was huger slaughter of heroes,' says the poet, 'since Saxon and Angle from over the broad billow broke into Britain and harried the Welshman and, greedy for glory, got hold of the land.'

The victory marks the climax of the military achievement of Alfred's grandsons. Athelstan's rule was accepted from the Firth of Forth to the Channel, by the unconquered Northumbrians north of Tees, by the Norwegians and Danes of Yorkshire, the Midlands, and East Anglia, by the Mercians of the western Midlands, the Britons of Cornwall, and by his own West Saxons.

The lands north of the Humber retained their distinctive features down to and beyond the Norman Conquest, and broke away temporarily on Athelstan's death, but his valiant brothers, Edmund and Eadred, recovered and maintained the authority of the West Saxon dynasty over them, while his nephew, Edgar, was to reassert the lordship over the Celtic princes by a famous symbolic ceremony. In 973, according to a reliable tradition, he followed up his coronation by acting as steersman to a boat rowed on the River Dee by eight kings—Scottish, North British, Welsh, and Norse.

(IV) THE WEST SAXON SYSTEM OF GOVERNMENT

The reconquest of the Danelaw in the half-century that followed Alfred's death meant the extension of the West Saxon system of administration over all England south of the Humber. As regarded personal and private law, the right of men to follow their own native custom was taken for granted. The custom of Kent was in force for Kentishmen centuries after Kent had ceased to be a kingdom; the difference between the laws of the Mercians, the Danes, and the West Saxons was recognized as practically important in the twelfth century.

But in matters of public order and administration there had to be new regulations, and the laws and charters issued by Alfred's sons, grandsons, and great-grandsons indicate what was happening. At the beginning of the seventh century

Ethelbert of Kent had found it expedient to define the legal status of a new thing—the Christian Church; in the eighth century Ine had to deal with problems raised by the colonization of the Celtic south-west; in the tenth century West Saxon kings, with tasks of war and government necessitating new compulsions, with Danish and Mercian subjects who must be held by ties of interest and loyalty rather than by coercion, and with English subjects inured to violence and insecurity of property by years of warfare, were bound to legislate.

In drafting and issuing such laws the kings sought the aid of their 'wise men'—bishops, warriors, officials—in councils, held generally at some royal estate, all over Southern England, from Axminster to Faversham, from Lyminster to Whittlebury. Alfred, in one of his vivid similes, likens the various ways by which men seek wisdom to the different journeys men take to find the king's residence, where he is holding his moot, 'one by a long and bad and difficult road, one by a long but very direct and good road; one short and yet narrow and dirty, one short and smooth and good.' In the royal council the wise men might approve gifts of land as well as additions to the laws; they might plan campaigns; they might settle disputes between leading men.

But only a fraction of the work of government could be done at such central gatherings. In a thinly peopled country, with the inhabited regions separated from each other by wide belts of forest or marshland, the application of the laws had to depend on local activity. From the earliest times the Anglo-Saxons, like other Teutonic peoples, had used the method of adjusting difficulties and establishing rights in folk-moots— popular assemblies which freemen were bound to attend. When the demands of their rulers for tribute came to a district, it must have been in such assemblies that the distribution of the burden was worked out by the community.

The size and name of the districts themselves before the Danish invasions must be a matter of guesswork over a great part of England, though there are some facts for Kent and Wessex. By Alfred's time we can say that Wessex was divided into shires. These were probably sub-divided into smaller districts organized round royal estates or kings' *tuns*, supervised, for the collection of tribute, by royal reeves or stewards. The shires were under ealdormen, who led the forces of the shire against the Danes in Alfred's wars.

When Mercia, East Anglia, and the Danelaw were subdued they also were organized by shires, some, as in Norfolk, Suffolk, and Essex, corresponding to older districts. In the Midlands, however, there was probably a drastic remodelling of local units, determined to some extent, it would seem, by Danish practices. The Midland shires take their names from the towns on which they centre, and some, like Leicestershire, and Cambridgeshire without the Isle of Ely, are almost symmetrical round their county towns. It seems most likely that these were the districts settled by 'the armies which belonged' to Leicester and to Cambridge. Broadly speaking, it is true to say that the divisions on which our county government to-day is based had been laid down over the greater part of England by the time of Athelstan.

The lesser districts into which the new shires were divided have, on the other hand, been obsolete for many years. It is not till the third quarter of the century that they are officially described as 'hundreds,' but the activities connected with them were certainly at work under Edward and Athelstan. Where the district was new, it represented a hundred taxable units, and everywhere it had a monthly law court and its inhabitants bore a joint responsibility for catching thieves. In Wessex and Kent the local variations in size and taxability suggest the adaptation of existing divisions to a new purpose, but north of the Thames everything indicates the imposition by authority of a new system that involved drastic reorganization.

War and migration had inevitably produced lawlessness and disrespect for property, and the regulations whereby the men of the hundred were bound to deal with thieves, and the hundred reeves were ordered to assist each other in pursuing them, were not the only royal decrees designed to enforce law and order.

In spite of the destruction they brought with them, the

Danish invasions stimulated the growth of towns. The walled and garrisoned town offered security, both for storing movable property and for trading transactions, and the tenth-century kings encouraged their growth by various regulations, designed to prevent the sale of stolen property and to facilitate the collection of royal tolls. Sales must take place in 'boroughs,' and before official witnesses, and a special penalty for breach of the borough peace safeguarded the salesman and purchaser.

The relations of the Danes with Scandinavia, with Ireland, and with the Continent, where a 'Danelaw' had been established at the mouth of the Seine in 911, stimulated the traffic at the ports and up the rivers as far as ships could go; York, Grimsby, Ipswich, London, and even inland towns, like Norwich, Thetford, and Cambridge, are examples of the response to these influences. The centring of the shire on the 'county town' also brought custom with it; whereas some shire moots assembled at a stone or on a heath, in many of the new shires the mootstow was in the town that gave its name to the county, as at Cambridge, Northampton, or Worcester.

But the special concerns of the towns, whether connected with sales or tolls or breaches of the borough peace, made it advisable for them to have their own tribunals, and by 975 the laws recognize at least three kinds of court, the shire moot, the hundred moot, and the borough moot.

In all these moots the law was declared, the procedure directed, and the issue decided by the men of the moot, that is, by those who were bound to attend it, whether they were personally concerned with the cases before the court or not. Undoubtedly social inequalities were reflected in the outcome of discussions, and matters were decided by the more important men present, but the action taken was that of the community, whether shire or hundred.

Danish influence, here also, was working. The great Icelandic Sagas have immortalized Scandinavian litigiousness, compounded almost equally from a sense of fair play and a sense of one's own rights; and the fact that the Scandinavian word *Law* has completely ousted the native English term bears lasting witness to the reinforcement given by our ninth-century settlers to the Anglo-Saxon habit of regarding both legal rights and legal courts as primarily the concern of the people rather than of their rulers.

It would appear that the Danelaw was socially more equalitarian than the old West Saxon kingdom, and we hear more of the 'doomsmen' of the courts in the Midlands than south of the Thames. But the evidence is scanty: the very fact that so much was settled by illiterate freemen has deprived us of the records which would enable us to describe proceedings in the courts of tenth- and eleventh-century England with the detail that is possible in France and Italy, the countries of written law.

The law which regulated personal rights, whether of Danes or English, was folk-law, but the wars had inevitably magnified the part played by the king in enforcing it. Alfred, Edward, Athelstan, and Edgar were all concerned with the problem of enforcing order. The king's peace, once a matter that affected the king's personal dignity and safety, and those persons or places who enjoyed the special privilege of his protection, was coming to cover a wider and wider field, just as the tie of personal loyalty which had linked the king's companions and thegns to him was being extended to cover the safety and honour of the whole nation.

'King Edward exhorted his wise men at Exeter that they should all search out how their peace might be better than it had been. He asked who would apply himself to its amendment, and be in that fellowship that he was, and love that which he loved and shun that which he shunned.' Athelstan's approval was asked and given for a thoroughgoing scheme worked out by the bishops and reeves who owned land in Middlesex and Surrey, the regions belonging to London, for the joint protection of their property against thieves, especially cattle thieves.

This London peace gild is one of the earliest examples of that fruitful partnership between voluntary association and governmental support of which English history affords so many examples, down to the East India Company, the British Medical Association, and the Charity Organization Society.

(volutions + progressions)

The king recognizes the legal standing of the gild, its system of mutual insurance against theft, its right to fine the slack member. But the express object of the gild is to make more effective the laws approved in three recent royal councils.

In all the moots, though the judgment was given by the body of the court, its execution depended on the co-operation of the presiding official, who was there to see to the collection of the king's share of the money penalties, due to him by ancient custom, or of the newer fines incurred for disobedience to his decrees, or breach of his extended peace. Thus it was to the interest of king and litigant alike that the powers of the king should be brought into play to secure that the judgment given by the men of shire or hundred should be, in fact, executed. A strong, just, peace-loving king had a temporal as well as a moral reward if he concerned himself in these matters.

Alfred's great grandson, Edgar the Peaceable, who reigned from 959 to 975, was the last Anglo-Saxon king effectively to embody this conception. 'I, Edgar,' he says in one charter, 'have been exalted as king over the English nation by God's grace, and He has now reduced beneath my sway Scots and Cumbrians, and likewise Britons and all that this island contains, so that I now occupy my throne in peace.' No military triumphs marked his reign, but his successors looked back to his laws as the standard of good government; the chroniclers told of the eight kings who did him honour at Chester, and ecclesiastical writers cherished his name as the great ally of the Church and patron of the refounded monasteries.

His coronation, deferred until he was thirty, is the first for which an order of service exists, and includes the rite of unction, expressing the religious aspect of the royal office.

'Kings remote, greatly honoured, to the king submitted,' says the Anglo-Saxon chronicler. 'Was no fleet so insolent, no host so strong, that in the Angle race took from him aught, the while the noble king ruled on the royal seat.' But when his child succeeded to the kingdom 'a babe ungrown,' 'God's adversaries God's law brake; and monasteries destroyed and monks expelled; and ever afterwards it greatly grew in evil.'

(v) THE DANISH CONQUEST
(975–1042)

The murder of Edgar's elder son in the interest of the younger and the grabbing of monastic lands by greedy officials were sure signs of the internal unsoundness of the kingdom, and as epidemics seize on a debilitated population, so the Scandinavian invaders descended again upon England before two years had passed. The history of the sixty years from Edgar's death to the accession of Edward the Confessor in 1042 is a bitter sequel to the heroic struggle of Alfred's days.

Weakness on the throne, and treachery at the council and in the field, left England vulnerable to the planned attacks of a unified Scandinavian monarchy. Over against the heroic loyalties of the ealdormen Byrhtnoth and his following at Maldon in 991 must be set the treachery of other ealdormen, the purchased truces and the shameful massacre of Danish civilians ordered by King Æthelred on St. Brice's Day in 1002, on the pretext of a suspected plot.

Swein, the Danish king, retaliated with more savage raids, landing in Norfolk, Kent, Devon, and Hampshire, and driving inland into the heart of the country. 'Then were the wise men summoned to the king to give counsel how this country could be defended. But though something was then resolved, it stood not even for a month; at last there was not a chief man who would gather a force, but each fled as he best might; nor even at last would any shire assist another.'

In 1012 the Danes murdered their prisoner, Archbishop Aelfheah of Canterbury, for his refusal to pay the ransom they demanded. Finally, in 1013, Swein came prepared for conquest. The men of the Danelaw, from Northumberland to Hertfordshire, accepted him as their king willingly; hostages were taken from the Western Midlands; and when London submitted, Ethelred the ill-advised fled from the country.

From 1013 to 1042 England was ruled by Danish kings; by Swein, by his son, Cnut, and by Cnut's two sons, Harold and Harthacnut. Ethelred's son, Edmund Ironside, made a valiant recovery of ground and morale in 1016, but his treaty with Cnut was followed in a month by his death.

Humiliating as it might seem, this subjection to Danish rule was probably the best that could befall England in the circumstances. England was once more under one ruler, and that a strong ruler. It became temporarily one of a group of kingdoms that made up a Scandinavian empire; it enjoyed peace and security, and Cnut proved himself a respecter both of the law and the religion of England. He even married Ethelred's widow, the Norman Emma.

There was no breach of continuity in government. The moots met as before, the king maintained the rights and accepted the obligations of the English monarchy, and, like his West Saxon predecessors, bestowed lands and privileges on the English monasteries. It is true that England became a tempting prize to Cnut's Scandinavian rivals; the threat of invasion and conquest from across the North Sea was almost continuous down to twenty years after the Norman Conquest. But, in fact, England lost little and gained a precious breathing space of peace and order, even if no solid or lasting addition to her governmental resources was made.

If the upkeep of the fleet required by Cnut's sea-linked dominions meant heavy financial burdens for the English, they gained advantages from the commercial connections that his rule opened up. Danish magnates, who familiarized the country with the title *jarl* or earl, held high office over the English; a royal bodyguard of professional soldiers held a privileged position, but Englishmen also held governmental posts. English learning and religion continued to flourish—'Merry sang the monks at Ely as Cnut the king rowed by.'

Thus when Cnut's empire went to pieces on his death, and his two sons, unable to hold their assigned positions, proved short-lived, the way was open for a return to the line of Alfred. Cnut had welcomed Ethelred's son, his own stepson, Edward, at his court; now, in 1042, 'all the people received Edward for king, as was his natural right.'

CHAPTER IV

ENGLAND UNDER THE LAST ANGLO-SAXON KING
(1042–1066)

IN Ethelred's youngest son, Edward the Confessor, the direct line of Egbert ended. Not until 1154 did a descendant of Edgar again sit on the throne of England, and though an Englishman then hailed Henry II as the corner stone which bound together the two walls of the English and the Norman races, the Anglo-Saxon strain in him was well submerged by Norman, Flemish, and Angevin blood.

In the days to come 'the laws of Edward the Confessor' was to become a sacrosanct phrase. King after king swore at his coronation to uphold them, until the rationalists of 1688 deleted the clause from the coronation oath. No enactments of Edward's reign exist, and the tract that bears that name is the work of a twelfth-century antiquarian.

But there is ample material for reconstructing the system of law and government under which Englishmen lived in his days, the system, which, by the first of a long series of constitutional fictions, the Norman conqueror promised to preserve unaltered when he claimed himself to be the lawful heir, by hereditary right, of the Confessor. This is the moment at which to survey the English scene as a whole, before Norman influence is brought to bear upon it, and to ask what forces were working in and holding together English society.

The custom of the people, the power of the great men, the authority of the monarchy, and the persistent and omnipresent action of the Christian Church; these made and governed the common life of the nation.

(1) CUSTOMARY LAW

The custom of the people was still declared and applied in the people's moots, which assembled monthly for the hundred, thrice a year for the borough, and twice a year for the shire, and met all the normal needs of men, who sought the wider publicity of the shire moot for establishing permanent titles to land, but found the hundred most generally adequate for what would now be described as criminal matters. The presiding official in the shire was now generally a shire-reeve; since it had become usual for one ealdorman to take charge of several shires, some of his duties were discharged by a less eminent man who looked to him for some matters, but was the king's deputy, and more and more frequently received letters or 'writs' from the king addressed to him and the shire bishop, containing information or commands to be communicated to the men of the shires. Sometimes a royal messenger might attend the moot, but it was still the folk moot, declaring folk law and responsible for the action taken in response to the royal message.

The justice done in these moots, primitive and even barbaric as its methods might be called by those accustomed to modern techniques, was in accordance with the public opinion of the community. The oath-helpers who swore before God that a party was telling the truth were going on their knowledge of their neighbour's character; they risked the commission of a mortal sin if they misjudged him. The doomsmen could give the advantage in procedure to the men with the good reputation; the officiating priest could mitigate the rigour of the ordeal for a man in whose innocence he was confident. Ordeal and compurgation might be bound up with a naïve faith in miracles, but they also had a close relation with human commonsense.

By the time of Edward the Confessor, the presiding reeve in many of the hundred courts represented not the king but some great churchman or layman. Kings seeking to reward faithful servants or to endow some monastery or bishopric had given away their financial interests in the hundred court—the 'profits of justice'—as being the most readily available wealth that they could bestow, and it was the thegn's or bishop's or abbot's agent who received the money penalties accruing to the king from the loser in the lawsuit or the breaker of the law.

Three of the twelve hundreds of Worcestershire were under the bishop; St. Albans Abbey was responsible for one of the Hertfordshire hundreds, and Edward the Confessor, distressed, according to monastic tradition, at the poor food supplied in the abbey refectory to his young kinsmen who followed religion in St. Edmund's Abbey, bestowed on it his rights in the eight and a half hundreds of West Suffolk, still administered to-day by a separate county council, and held in Cnut's days by Edward's mother, Emma. But whether the profits of the hundred court went to king or to subject, it was the men of the hundred who declared the law and determined which party should find the proof and by what means.

In the smallest community, the township, custom and the common consent of the villagers regulated the methods of cultivation of the fields and times of sowing and harvesting. This was true both in the villages where freemen worked on their own holdings, and in those where a great man owned the village, and the villagers spent a fixed share of their time in working on his *in-land*, and caring for his stock. Agricultural practices varied according to local customs or local conditions, but in general even the serf or the half-free man could claim the protection of the public opinion of his own community, while the lord's share of the village arable and woodland and pasture was subject to the same customary time-table of ploughing, fencing, mowing, and grazing as those of the workers, whose smaller shares were contiguous with his in the open ploughed fields or fenced water meadows, and whose beasts grazed with his on the common pasture.

The villages of small freemen were commoner in the Danelaw, and the villages dominated by one great man were commoner in the south-west, but no rule can be laid down save that where enterprising wood-cutters and squatters brought newly cleared woodland under cultivation, the new community was likely to be lordless and independent.

(ii) The Aristocracy

The custom of the people had from the earliest days consecrated inequality. Every freeman had his rights, but the rights differed for different men. The damages that could be claimed for wrong doing, like the sort of evidence needed to prove wrong doing, were graded according to social status, varying from Kent to Mercia, from Wessex to the Danelaw. As a writer of Edward's days said: 'People and law went by ranks'; and the difference between the man whose death must be atoned for by twelve hundred shillings, and the "twy hynd" men whom it only cost two hundred shillings to slay, was a difference that ran through the whole structure of Anglo-Saxon society. The rights, the powers, and the functions of the leading men are of essential importance to an understanding of eleventh-century England.

Rank was hereditary, but not rigidly so. Men could rise or sink in the social order by chance, by effort, by crime, by royal favour. The oldest, and a continuing cause for eminence, was royal favour; those bound to the king by ties of faith and loyalty, who did him service on the battlefield or in his household, had honour and rewards in accordance.

To the old warband of invasion days there corresponded the king's thegns, some, perhaps, the descendants of those who had fought under Alfred, some of more recent merit and reward. A king's thegn had his legal status; he had lands, sometimes very extensive, but in any case enough to make a moderately sized village, and with the land, as we have seen, there went normally rights to the labour necessary for its exploitation. He would probably exercise some sort of judicial supervision over and responsibility for the dwellers on his land, and over the men who had sought his protection; he might hold a royal charter or book granting him royal financial privileges—toll, market, or judicial profits.

Such men were, in fact, a local aristocracy, a local ruling class. At a higher level the ealdormen, since the days of Cnut called *jarls* or earls, had power based both on office and on land; their holdings might be scattered over many shires, as might those of the king's great household officials. These men, summoned by the king to his councils, were an indispensable element in the government; by their advice, and by that of his bishops, the king had to make his practical decisions in face of danger from abroad or rebellion at home, and their rivalries, with the separatist tendencies of the provinces over which they were set, make up much of the politics of Edward's reign.

Harold, Godwine's son, king of England for nine months, earl of all the West Saxon shires south of the Thames, could count on the support of his two brothers, earls of the East Anglian and South Midland shires; whilst the earls of the rival house of Leofric ruled over the shires between the Welland and the Tyne. To the power that office and lands gave such men was added the social and economic influence derived from the judicial privileges granted them by the king in their own estates, and from the personal links that bound to their service the many men who were commended to them and looked to them for protection and justice.

Such men constituted a ruling class, but not a caste. Successful commercial enterprise as well as royal favour might make a man 'worthy of thegn-right'; the great might lose wealth or office by a judgment of the king's council, like Harold's elder brother, Sweyn. Inability to pay a judicial money penalty might involve lowering of status or even loss of freedom.

Colonization, conquest, internal warfare, no less than economic change, had prevented the establishment of static social conditions, and the last of these shattering impacts from abroad was in its turn to effect a transformation, when the coming of the Normans would impose a new pattern on English society even more important than the new ingredient they brought to the population. A hundred and eleven years after the Battle of Hastings a writer could say that, apart from the peasantry, it was impossible to tell an Englishman from a Norman; but the change from Anglo-Saxon thegn to Norman baron had been final and irrevocable.

(iii) The Monarchy

In eleventh-century England there was as yet no one law: local custom divided one district from another as much as did the rivalries of great men. For centuries the monarchy and the Church had been the unifying forces. The king was not only the leader in war and the defender of the realm against the invader, the overlord of subject kings, the conqueror imposing a nation-wide framework of administration within which diverse customs could function. As the ruler, sworn by the Church to uphold justice and order, whose peace extended over the whole realm, and as the fountain of honour and precedence, the lord who could claim the faith of all his subjects, he was holding together forces that threatened to split England into a second heptarchy.

Edward the Confessor might fall far short of his ancestors' greatness, but throughout the kingdom his reeves collected the tolls, the gelds, the profits of justice that were his royal due, his writs were read and respected in the moots, his thegns and ealdormen assembled at his summons to take counsel for the whole nation in his presence. The Anglo-Saxon kings had solid assets as well as undeveloped potentialities to bequeath to their Norman successors.

Again, whilst the evolution of English customary law and of the English ruling class had proceeded in almost complete isolation from continental developments, the English monarchy and, above all, the English Church had been active agents in maintaining contacts with Europe, both personal and technical. Edward the Confessor himself was of mixed descent and foreign upbringing. His mother Emma was the sister of a Norman duke and from the age of twelve to thirty-six he had lived in Normandy. Freeman's famous book begins the Norman Conquest in 1042 rather than in 1066. England had never been isolated from the Continent; literary, religious, commercial, and matrimonial connections had been maintained uninterruptedly from the time when Ethelbert of Kent took a Frankish princess to wife, and modelled his household on a Merovingian pattern. Egbert had been a refugee in Frankish territory in the days when Offa corresponded with Charlemagne. Alfred had married his daughter to the Count of Flanders. Athelstan's sisters had become wives to Charles the Simple of the second royal line of France, to Hugh of Paris, ancestor of the third French line and to the Emperor Otto I. Athelstan himself had been a European figure, in touch with the direct

rulers of Europe, and receiving at his court fugitives driven
from their homes by the Danes.

Cnut had dominated Scandinavia and the northern seas,
and had used his commanding position to renew contacts with
southern Europe, corresponding with the ruler of Aquitaine,
attending the coronation of the Emperor Conrad at Rome, and
securing from him and other southern princes privileges and
protection for English pilgrims and merchants travelling to
Italy. His marriage to Emma, Ethelred's widow, had put him
in close touch with Normandy. Edward the Confessor's sister
had married a Norman count and their son had been given an
English earldom, whilst William himself had been welcomed
as his cousin's guest in England fifteen years before his forces
landed at Pevensey in 1066.

(IV) THE ANGLO-SAXON CHURCH

Even stronger and more persistent than that of the monarchy
had been the influence of the Church in making for the unification of the English people, and in linking England with Europe.
The fifth-century invasions had severed direct connection with
the Continent, but indirect relations had been maintained
through Ireland and Iona. When the envoys of Gregory the
Great arrived at Canterbury in 597, they reopened a channel
of communication that was never closed again. A succession
of evangelists and ecclesiastical organizers followed in the foot-
steps of Augustine; the Italian Paulinus who proceeded to
Northumbria, the Burgundian Felix, apostle of East Anglia,
the Frank Angilbert whose 'barbarian tongue highly offended'
the West Saxon king, so that he secured the help of an English
assistant bishop and Angilbert went home, to become bishop
of Paris. Most notable of all, the Greek Theodore of Tarsus with
his assistant, the African Abbot Hadrian, was sent from Rome
by the Pope in 669, when deaths from pestilence had increased
the confusion in the Church caused by the divergence between
the usages of Rome and of Iona.

It was a two-way traffic; Wilfrid, who championed the
Roman discipline at Whitby in 664, had spent five years at
Rome, whither Benedict Biscop, the nobly born founder and

abbot of Jarrow, made five journeys, bringing back relics, vestments, stained glass, pictures, and, above all, the books which gave Bede his learning. English girls went overseas to monasteries, whence some returned to marry princes or rule English abbeys, while others remained there to become abbesses where they had been pupils, a career which Hilda of Whitby only just missed. Ceolfrid of Wearmouth, Bede's beloved father abbot, whose resignation and departure on the long journey to Rome he describes most movingly, was only one of many old pilgrims who, with their life work done, made for Rome as a homing bird seeks its nest.

But soon the travellers were setting out with a wider purpose. Within a century of the conversion of Kent, Englishmen were taking the lead in the attack on European paganism. Wilfrid, the stormy petrel of Northumbria, had tried in vain to convert the Frisians before he succeeded in converting the South Saxons, and the missionary campaign of the eighth century was fairly launched by the hermit Egbert, who inspired a succession of evangelists to carry the word to the heathen of Germany, 'whence the Angles and Saxons are said to have derived their origin.'

The first archbishop of the missionary See of Utrecht was the Northumbrian Willibrord, ordained in 696. The West Saxon Winfrith or Boniface, who worked in Thuringia, Hesse, Saxony, and Bavaria, was consecrated 'bishop to the Germans' in 722 and archbishop in 732. He organized the German Church as Theodore had organized the English. Whether by policy or chance, Gregory the Great in bringing Christianity to England had created a force devoted to the service of the papacy; and Boniface was paying England's debt to Rome as he established Catholic discipline in the Frankish Church and carried the Gospel to those old Saxons whom he commended to the prayers of the English as of 'one blood and one bone with them.'

And the English gave labour as well as prayer; hosts of men and women came to work under him, and to serve as abbots, abbesses, and bishops of his new German abbeys and sees. He was throughout in the closest touch with his mother country, as with Rome, and when the obdurate Frisians murdered him in 754, the archbishop of Canterbury could write: 'The English people can rejoice in the midst of their grief to think that they have sent forth from Britain so great a scholar and so valiant a Christian soldier, with such a band of disciples for the salvation of so many souls.'

In the next generation, though the work of Boniface was carried on, the most notable Englishman in Europe came from another kingdom and worked in another field, as a missionary of culture. A pupil of Bede's pupil Egbert, Alcuin, the master of the School of York which had ousted Jarrow from the first place in Northumbrian scholarship, was persuaded by Charlemagne, who met him in Italy in 781, to come to the Frankish court. There he became head of the palace school, friend and tutor of Charles himself, and finally abbot of St. Martin's of Tours, making it a great centre of learning.

Eighty years after his death, Alfred, seeking to restore the good learning shattered by the Danes, asked and obtained the services of Frankish as well as Mercian and Welsh scholars; the archbishop of Reims sent him Grimbald of St. Omer and John the Old Saxon. The stream of culture was flowing back again, and the art and calligraphy of England in the tenth century clearly show continental influence. So does the monastic revival of Edgar's days; Dunstan in exile in Flanders, Oswald at Fleury on the Loire, had felt the impulses of the reform movements of Lorraine and Burgundy.

Backed by Edgar, these men, with Aethelwold of Abingdon and Winchester, refounded abbeys destroyed or abandoned in the Danish wars, or founded new ones[1]. Further, they brought to bear on the active life of the Church the influence of pastors and bishops reared in these surroundings. As always, religion went hand in hand with good learning. New centres of art, scholarship, and culture arose, as at Winchester, Canterbury, and Peterborough, rivalling or surpassing the Northumbrian abbeys of earlier days. For the common man of those days and for the future of the mother tongue, the most significant literary figure

---

[1] See below, pp. 125-127.

was Aelfric, abbot of Cerne and Eynsham, a pupil of the cathedral school at Winchester.

Aelfric, like Bede, spent most of his life within the walls of a monastery, but he wrote for laymen, not monks; using the English tongue to speak to all and sundry for their edification and salvation. Alfred had been a pioneer translator, struggling to find the words for the thought and arguments of an alien idiom; Aelfric writes with the rhythm and balance of a great preacher. Whether he is re-telling a Bible story, relating the passion of a saint, or exhorting to virtue, he is linking up the learning of the Latin scholar with the needs of the practical Christian and, in the process, teaching the English language its own powers.

Another great homilist, Archbishop Wulfstan, whose sermon to the English nation in the year 1014 told them how thoroughly they had deserved to be conquered by Cnut, lacks Aelfric's literary range, but may fairly be called the author of the first great political oration recorded in the mother tongue. The archbishop, indeed, exemplifies the constant influence of the Church on English government and law. Where unwritten custom had to be supplemented by written decrees, the clergy as the writing class necessarily had a hand in drafting them, and Wulfstan's style can clearly be traced in the wording of Aethelred's laws. Bishops and priests were thus not only giving counsel but determining forms; besides assenting to legislation and approving royal grants of land or privileges, they framed the documents by which such gifts were conveyed, thus consciously or unconsciously infusing English legal transactions with Roman traditions.

Again, the close contacts of a loyal Church with Rome affected political thinking. It was the Anglo-Saxon Boniface who had anointed the first Carolingian king by papal authority in 751, and when Dunstan in 973 introduced the coronation order with the Frankish ceremony of unction imposed upon the older usages of election, acclamation, and crowning, he was, in fact, expressing the papal attitude to kingship; at once an exaltation of its dignity by consecration, an emphasis of its moral obligation by the terms of the royal precept, and an assumption by the Church of the responsibility for watching over the fulfilment of the duty there undertaken by the crowned and anointed king. The new rite was the definition and endorsement by the Church of those functions of kingship which Alfred had accepted from the past and enlarged by his actions.)

Thus the Anglo-Saxons who, unlike the Goths and the Franks, had never lived under the provincial administration of imperial Rome, were from the seventh century onwards subject to a continuous stream of indirect Roman influence through ecclesiastical channels. Every Latinist who served the king or taught the people was informing native traditions with something that came from an older and more sophisticated society. Africa in the last hundred years has had a similar experience when served by evangelists who, like Mary Slessor, became judges and experts in African law, or by chiefs who, like Aggrey, used a European education to incorporate the native with the Christian culture.

Merchants voyaging across the North Sea, envoys carrying diplomatic messages, scholars and pilgrims, clergy carrying the alms of the faithful to Rome, archbishops seeking the papal gift of the pallium, all these came and went between England and the Continent. Whatever the Norman Conquest brought to England, it was not the rediscovery of a forgotten outlying region, nor did it bring an isolated and semi-barbarous kingdom in touch with a higher civilization. English ways were not those of Normandy or the empire, but in her literature, her art, and her religion England had a living and fruitful native tradition that acknowledged its debt to Rome; her monarchy was heir to the achievements and obligations of great men, and her native law and custom was so deeply rooted as to compel acceptance by Danish and Norman conqueror in succession as the standard of good government.

In the six hundred years that had gone by since the Roman legions left Britain, the English people had come into being. In the bitter quarrel between Godwine and his opponents in 1052-3, actual civil war was avoided because, as the Anglo-Saxon chronicler says, 'It was hateful to them that they should fight against men of their own race, because there were very few who were worth much on either side who were not Englishmen.' Behind the title, 'Edward by the grace of God, King of the English,' lies an unwritten story of efforts and achievements by sundry men working on divers tasks; by the colonists who planted their settlements along the river banks, pushing up the valleys into the heart of the country, gaining ground on the woodlands, generation by generation, as the larger communities sent out daughter townships, and isolated villages enlarged their bounds till the no man's land had to be partitioned; by the traders, venturing along old ridgeway or Roman road to sell their goods at the market centre, or crossing the sea to fetch wares from Frisia, from Norway, or Ireland; by the warrior kings, forced by a common menace to form ties of federation or overlordship, to impose military or financial demands, to undertake the task of imposing order and securing justice; by the Christian teachers bringing their lore of mercy and loving-kindness to fill out the noble pagan code of honour and loyalty, bringing hope to mitigate pagan gloom, and bringing the delights of learning and the sense of membership in a larger commonwealth to spur on men's efforts to build on the old foundations and to advance the purposes of kings and popes. All of these, the men who fought, the men who prayed, and the men who laboured, had, by their response to the challenge of hardness, of danger, of distance, and of the invader, made possible the cultural ascendancy of Northumbria, the military and commercial ascendancy of Mercia, and the transformation of the ninth-century West Saxon ascendancy into the national monarchy of the house of Alfred. King and people alike had held the customs of the community as a trust for posterity, to be preserved and therefore, when necessary, modified.

Each man had his place in eleventh-century society and knew his fellows' place; each man had his rights in law and recognized the rights of others; and through their mother-tongue, disciplined and developed by generations of scholars to be a vehicle for rational thought as well as for daily speech or festal song, the English people were becoming articulate.

CHAPTER V

THE NORMAN CONQUEST

SEEING that the English had accomplished so much for themselves, how was it that they were unable to drive off or drive out William of Normandy and the heterogeneous army, recruited from half a dozen French provinces, which landed at Pevensey on 28th September, 1066? Why, in fact, was there a Norman Conquest?

Personal, political, and military factors all entered into the situation. Edward the Confessor had no children. Fifteen years before his death he had indicated as his heir William of Normandy, his kinsman on the mother's side, and had appointed a Norman archbishop of Canterbury to make the succession safer.

The violent anti-Norman reaction thus provoked had helped to establish the dominating influence among his great men of his father-in-law, Godwine, and of Godwine's four sons, whose power as landowners and administrators extended over most of England south of the Trent. When Edward died in December 1065, Harold, Godwine's son, seemed to the council of the nation better fitted to defend the realm against the double threat from Norway and Normandy than Edward's young great-nephew, Edgar.

Practical needs were of more concern than royal blood, and the fact that Harold himself had in the past sworn to uphold William's claims, though it won William the support of the pope, did not lose Harold any English support. Harold's valiant and successful September campaign in the north against the Norwegian invaders exhausted English military resources, so that he had only the militia of the southern shires to back up his household troops at Hastings in October.

But the Norman Conquest meant more than the victory of Hastings; more than the skilfully planned march of William's army along the coast, avoiding the hazards of the Weald, from Canterbury up the Thames valley to Wallingford, from Wallingford along the Icknield Way, till at Berkhamsted the Londoners, recognizing their isolation, came with the bishops and aldermen and the young Edgar to accept William as king; more even than his coronation by the ancient English rites on Christmas Day in Westminster Abbey.)

The mere military conquest took not three months, but five years; risings in Devon, Cornwall, Somerset, Dorset, Yorkshire, Herefordshire, and Cheshire had to be put down; supporting raids from Denmark and Norway in Kent, East Anglia, and Lindsey had to be beaten off. Not till Yorkshire had been finally reduced to quiescence by devastation of a thoroughness unknown since Alfred's days, and Hereward's stronghold in the Isle of Ely had surrendered in 1071, was the fighting over. But even that does not constitute the Norman Conquest. How was William able to hold and pass on to his heirs a kingdom which Swein and his descendants had only kept for twenty-six years?

What William of Normandy brought was not necessarily of higher intrinsic quality than what he found in England, but it met certain outstanding needs of the time. English institutions were adequate for local requirements, but there was no machinery to secure concerted action on a national scale when need arose, or to apply effective coercion to the disloyal servant of the ruler. Local autonomies and patriotisms were reflected in a diversity of social, political, and legal customs; no co-ordinating force existed to weld them into a national system. Above all, the fighting forces could not meet the demand of warfare as eleventh-century Europe knew it, in spite of the Danish kings' innovations. The Normans were establishing their reputation as the most effective fighters and the most efficient governors in the Western world, and William was a typical Norman. He had established his authority against the long odds of youth and illegitimacy in his own duchy of Normandy, and made it about the best governed fief in France. In him the violence of Viking ancestors was controlled by a respect for law common to Danes and Englishmen, with a liking for order natural to the heir of blended Norse and Carolingian traditions of government. He had to have the law on his side. Where his father had seized the woman he wanted, careless of title, William, equally determined to have his will, desired a lawful wife, and secured in the end the blessing of the Church, with the help of the best canon lawyer of his duchy and at the price, cheerfully paid, of founding two monasteries in his favourite city of Caen.

So in England he was determined to have and to hold every right that Edward his predecessor had had, but with that went recognition of others' rights. Those who had resisted their lawful king were rebels, but the citizens of London who had submitted were assured their ancient customs and property rights in the charter they still cherish at the Guildhall; bishoprics and abbeys kept their ancient lands and liberties, and if a Norman newcomer encroached on them, the memory of the country-side, voiced by the shire moot, was evoked to declare what those rights were under the laws of Edward the Confessor.

I

Though in so many respects a conservative, in one field William broke with the past decisively. The military technique that he brought was that of the mounted knight and the fortified castle, both new to England, and both indispensable elements in the military conquest of the country. His victories were pegged down by the building of castles from Dover to Exeter, from the Tower of London to York.

The mounted knights, practised in up-to-date continental discipline, whose training during the weeks of waiting at St. Valery for a fair wind had enabled William to win the battle of Hastings, were to be the military basis of his power in England. The means by which they were provided were to transform English social organization, and to constitute a principal unifying force in Anglo-Norman law and government. The Conqueror, in rewarding his followers with the lands and lordships of the English resisters, made it a condition that the holder should provide a fixed quota of properly equipped knights to serve in his army every year.

The bargain between the king and the chief land holders involved a series of lesser bargains, whereby the magnates made sure that they would have the knights to supply. Sometimes they kept them under their roof, sometimes they granted them a holding to live on. It was through these series of contracts that the so-called feudal system[1] came into existence; that chain of defined relationships of obligation and subordination, that standardized set of rules of service and tenure, that established code of conduct and ethics which replaced the varying practices and undefined understandings of Anglo-Saxon society.

A business-like definition of responsibility at every level linked up the villager at the bottom, who held his strips of cultivable land as a condition of working on his lord's estate, through the knight, who held that estate on condition of service in the king's army, with the magnate, who called up the knight when the king demanded his quota of ten or twenty or fifty knights. All men held of the king, directly or indirectly, and by this the Anglo-Norman king had secured a hold over his great men which no Anglo-Saxon king had had. For if the tenant broke the contract, the land was forfeit, and the king could keep it or give it to another, as William did when earls like Waltheof of Huntingdon, Ralph of East Anglia, and Roger of Hereford plotted against him in 1075.

On this foundation of the military obligation of the land holder rested a social and political structure which incorporated the traditions of both England and Normandy. Under the ethical code of honour and trust between lord and man it was the lord's duty to see that his man had justice, and the man's duty to give his lord counsel and aid, giving judgment with his peers in his lord's presence, as the freemen had been accustomed to give judgment in shire and hundred court.

Through these mutual duties a large part of the necessary

[1] The adjective *feudal* was coined by a French historian of the seventeenth century from the Latin *feudum* (French *fief*), the word used for that holding of land in respect of which the tenant owed his specific service and dues.

work of government was carried on. All over Norman England feudal courts were held for the military tenants, at which the countless problems of adjusting rights and duties between old custom and new needs were handled, as they came up, by the Norman and English dependants of the lords of the fiefs. There was no break with the past in law; the desire of the new king to be accepted as the lawful heir of Edward the Confessor operated to preserve old custom, and the practical necessity of living by the land made the new landlords accept the agrarian practice of the men who knew the land, the men by whose labours alone the land could support them.

The village court was now the lord's manor court, for his free and unfree tenants, but the villagers took part in its judgments, and there was no transformation of the different types of village community into one uniform manorial pattern. The English peasants, generally speaking, became less free, but slavery tended to disappear. The great landowner was usually, but not always, a Norman. Englishmen and Normans alike lived by old English custom and new Norman theory, applied with a consistency that conquest alone could have made possible.

The king's central court or council is the outstanding instance of this dual aspect of the Conqueror's government. Like the court he had held as duke of Normandy, it was composed of his vassals and officials, but as the earls and bishops who had attended the 'meetings of the wise men' under Edward were now royal vassals holding their lands by knight service, to the English chronicler the sessions of the king's court were meetings of the 'Wise Men'—the Witan.

William may well have been following an English tradition in holding the great assemblies at Christmas, Easter, and Whitsun at different centres; in using these sessions for doing justice and promulgating legislation he was making no new departure. The court served both as a feudal court at which the royal vassals gave judgment on each other, and as a royal tribunal at which the king might do justice to any subject who appealed to him, as the Anglo-Saxon kings had done.

The great officials of the household, like the royal clerks of

Edward the Confessor, were the king's own servants acting for him, when necessary, in national matters, and though at first their offices were hereditary and feudal, at an early date the more important civil posts of the chamberlains, the chancellor, and the justiciar came to be held at the king's pleasure, in complete subordination to him. The king could not govern the country nor plan a campaign nor issue a decree that would be effectively observed unless he had the goodwill and co-operation of the leading royal vassals.

But he could not do justice to all men, as he had sworn to do at his coronation, unless he had efficient servants, and in the twenty years of William's reign, there are numerous instances of royal agents, with his full authority behind them, holding local sessions of the king's court to deal with the conflicting claims of natives and new-comers; in particular, with cases arising from the invasion of the rights of an English bishopric or abbey where a new Norman prelate often found himself in the position of trustee for an ancient foundation.

Further, the Norman duke's liking for order operated to make him a good man of business in financial matters. The material resources he inherited from Edward were exploited with a new efficiency. The royal income of Anglo-Saxon days, the tolls and tributes and the profits of justice, had been collected locally by the shire reeves and reeves of royal estates, and paid into a central treasury over which a royal treasurer ruled. William's household staff, like Edward's, acted as an un-differentiated central civil service, looking after his correspondence, his finances, and the running of the household; from it the later governmental departments were to develop. Here the feudal principle of the contract did not enter, and this central system was the potential antidote to the dangers inherent in feudalism. It was in effect the extension of the powers of kingship inherited from the Anglo-Saxon monarchy, reinforced by the military power of the new line. It was effectively linked with the shires twice over, by the sheriffs coming up to the king's court to pay in the royal revenues they had collected; by the royal envoys or justices going down from the king's court to administer his justice in the shire court, with the witness of the shire court often supplemented by the sworn information of a jury of local men.

The supreme instance of this interlocking is the great survey of 1086, planned at the royal council held at Gloucester at Christmas 1085, and recorded for posterity in the Domesday Book, still preserved at the Public Record Office. It is a monument of Norman thoroughness, exhibiting William's determination to secure a complete statement of the material assets of the country he had won, together with a statement of the title and the responsibility of the land holders. 'Who holds the land, what are its resources, and could more be made of them?' As the title derives both from pre-Conquest custom and from William's own gift the facts are attested both by Englishmen and Frenchmen serving on juries of the hundreds.

Similar inquiries may have been held before of individual estates, but nothing of the sort had been attempted before on a nation-wide scale. To the Englishmen inquiry into such minute details seemed indecent: 'It is shame to tell, though he thought it no shame to do. So very narrowly he caused it to be traced out that there was not one single hide or yard of land, not even an ox, nor a cow, nor a swine, that was not set down in writing.'

When all the aspects of the Domesday Inquest are considered, its scope both in space and time, covering, as it does, the state of England at three different dates; its checking of the findings of the sworn communal juries by information supplied by the feudal tenants; the investigation by the royal commissioners of disputed claims, and the registration of local custom where it affected the financial interests of the crown; perhaps the most convincing evidence of the capabilities of the government that planned and carried it out is the fact that the unwieldy mass of facts collected from the men of over thirty shires was reduced into two volumes of readily available information within a year of the inquiry, and has served as a work of reference, at first for administrators, later for historians, from that day to this.

The Norman Conquest is probably the most important event in English history; its results are still with us. It formed the traditions of our ruling class. To the earlier responsibility of the man for his neighbours was added the responsibility of the lord for his men and to his overlord. 'What the man owes to the lord, the lord owes to the man, save only deference.' And these responsibilities were rooted in the soil of England.

Land became the guarantee and the recompense of work done; military, judicial, administrative, agrarian. Further, it assured for good the commanding position of the monarchy. The strategic advantage given by the fact of conquest is only fully realized if we compare the nation-wide extension of the machinery controlled by William with the strict localization of that at the disposal of the contemporary kings of France. Only a small region round Paris was administered by officials under their orders; the great duchies and counties of France were governed, like Normandy, by the agents of the dukes and counts, not by the kings', and to build up the national monarchy, the French kings had to pursue a century-long policy of piece-meal annexation, resulting in the survival to our own days of deeply rooted provincialism.

In England, whatever powers the kings inherited and whatever organs of government they created were exercised over the whole realm. Much work might be left to the holders of fiefs, but no royal vassal could defy the king with impunity, and in every shire was a royal sheriff and one or more royal castles. By feudal law, applied more consistently in England than in any other European country, every rood of the land was held of the king, directly or indirectly. As inheritor of the monarchy of Alfred and Edgar, William had rights and duties which entitled him to concern himself with every man in the realm. He had sworn at his coronation to prevent violence and to see that justice was done to all; in the fulfilment of that oath by himself and by his successors, the whole programme for the development of the English monarchy was laid down.

II

At his coronation, William had also sworn to protect the rights of Holy Church. He had been an active patron of ecclesiastical reform in Normandy, and by continental standards there were some highly irregular church customs in England. The close interweaving of secular and religious activities had meant that there was little purely ecclesiastical machinery; the councils which issued ecclesiastical decrees were hardly distinguished from those which legislated in secular concerns, whilst the same men gave judgment on spiritual and temporal causes in the same courts. Moreover, the archbishop Stigand had been lawlessly intruded into the See of Canterbury to replace the Norman archbishop driven out in the anti-Norman movement of 1052, a fact that invalidated other appointments.

William had had the blessing of the Pope on his enterprise, and it was the Papal Legate who carried through the invidious work of cleaning up the episcopal bench for him. The new archbishop, Lanfranc, worked with William in complete sympathy, enforcing decency and order, according to the canon laws accepted in Europe, endeavouring to put down the insular custom of the marriage of parish clergy, transferring the bishops' seats from small villages to good-sized centres of population, and separating the courts where church law was enforced, from those where the men of the shire or the hundred declared the secular law. But when Pope Gregory VII attempted to establish a closer control over English affairs, by exacting homage from William, as if he, like his Norman kinsmen in Sicily, were a papal vassal, and when he demanded the attendance of English bishops at Rome, William took a firm line.

None of his predecessors had done homage to the Pope, nor would he; none of his bishops (who, unlike their Anglo-Saxon predecessors, were now royal vassals, paying homage and owing knight service for the lands of their sees) should leave his kingdom without his permission, or even, in the event of a papal schism, recognize either Pope as lawful until William gave the word. He would pay Peter's Pence as his predecessors had done; he was a good Christian; but he was master in his own house. Neither he nor his archbishop recognized that by accepting the standards of the canon law they were admitting a rival authority beyond their control. The disentangling of things spiritual from things temporal was

bound to produce in the future a conflict between the two
authorities competent to interpret the two laws.

III

If the effects of the Norman Conquest on English institutions were immeasurable, only second in importance were its
effects on the foreign relations of England. Its king was, with
a brief interruption from 1087 to 1096, to be duke of Normandy
down to its loss in 1204, and Normandy obstructed the kings
of France, both politically and geographically, in their long
struggle to establish an effective and not merely nominal
supremacy over the territory that stretched from the Channel
to the Mediterranean.

William's capital of Rouen blocked the lower Seine; and
when to the great Norman duchy he and his descendants added
Maine, Anjou, Poitou, and Aquitaine, their French lands far
exceeded in extent those directly ruled by the rulers of Paris.
Inevitably the French kings countered this threat by intriguing
with their heirs or rival claimants to the throne of England,
down to the times of Richard the Lionhearted, whose mighty
Chateau Gaillard on the lower Seine was a sword aimed
directly at the heart of the Île de France.

But Richard died and France breathed again. Philip
Augustus, stronger than any that came before him, summoned
his vassal John of England to answer in his court to the charges
brought against him by his own sub-vassals in Poitou, and
when he failed to appear, declared his fiefs forfeit, and in 1204
took Normandy by force of arms into his hands, thus severing
for two hundred and ten years the connection between England
and the opposite coast of the Channel.

The lands that John had inherited through his mother,
Eleanor, proved less easy to conquer. Poitou, the northern-most
part of Aquitaine, was taken by Philip's son from John's son
within ten years of John's death; but the districts south of the
Charente—Guienne and Gascony—continued to be a source
of discord for centuries. They were inhabited by a restless
nobility always ready to play off one king against another in
order to preserve their own independence. The treaty of 1259,

by which the English king surrendered his claims to Poitou and Normandy, and the French king accepted him as his vassal for Gascony and Guienne, seemed a statesmanlike compromise, but the settlement was not lasting. The feudal code that bound the vassal 'to love what his lord loved and loathe what he loathed, and never by word or deed do ought that should grieve him' became less and less practicable as the standard for regulating the relations between two national rulers. It was the marriage of John's great-grandson, Edward II, to a French princess that ultimately transformed the tension between English vassal and French overlord into the dynastic rivalry of two powerful monarchies, and launched the two nations on the fatal course of the Hundred Years' War, building up a tradition of national antagonism between Frenchmen and Englishmen that endured until the loss of Calais in 1558.

IV

New contacts with the Continent were bound to stimulate English trade, but there were other and more far-reaching economic effects of the Norman Conquest. It meant a wholesale transfer of land ownership, the introduction of a body of new-comers with new material demands, the establishment of new centres of population, and the wasting and de-population of certain regions. The Domesday Survey gives us some evidence of its short term effects on society and industry. The growth of town life was sharply accelerated. Merchants and craftsmen, gathering to supply the new types of goods required by the new ruling class, and to victual the new castles and abbeys, had added new suburbs to old towns and brought new towns into existence between 1066 and 1086.

Some regions had been laid waste during the Conquest; but others had been brought under cultivation for the first time or made more productive. The application of stricter legal theories and exacter definition to the relationship of lord and tenant resulted on the whole, it would seem, in a lowering of the status of the peasant. The fixing of responsibility for the land on the lord produces the assumption throughout Domesday Book that the normal agrarian unit is that of a lord with men working for him. The types of agricultural organization may vary widely, according to geographical and geological facts, and according to the racial traditions coming down from the past, but the village community that controls its own activities with no direction from above is hard to find, whilst the villagers' duties on their lords' lands seem to be on the increase and to be more strictly defined.

One result is that the difference between the country-side and the town becomes more marked. The embryonic industrial community cannot develop if restricted by such regulation, and the lords who want the goods that townsmen supply will have to release them from field labour. At first perhaps informally, but, as the twelfth century advances, by written deeds and charters, the king and other lords will recognize the privileged status of the borough, by permitting its inhabitants to organize themselves by associations for imposing rules of industry and trade, and to settle the special problems raised by trade and industry according to their own custom in courts of their own. The borough is young, as compared with the shire and the hundred, but its habit of settling its own affairs derives from the rural township. By 1086 there are already boroughs which have, for governmental purposes, the status of a hundred, and by the time of Henry II they are prepared to pay for the privilege of collecting themselves the dues owed to the crown, and paying them in at the royal treasury by an agent of their own choice.

It is only in the twelfth century, when the links with the Continent have been strengthened by Henry II's control of Anjou and Aquitaine, in addition to Normandy, that the full effects of the Norman Conquest on town life are seen. It is only in the twelfth and thirteenth centuries that its full effects on rural life are felt, with the advance in agrarian method and estate management, the increase in population, at once the cause and the consequence of the further advances of the plough on the woodland, and the advance in sheep-rearing and the production of wool both for export and for the native cloth industry.[1]

[1] For the effects of the Norman Conquest on the English monasteries see below, p. 128.

CHAPTER VI

THE ANGLO-NORMAN MONARCHY, 1087-1154: FROM TYRANNY TO ANARCHY

WILLIAM the Conqueror bequeathed to his sons a monarchy resting on the triple support of communal tradition, enshrined in the local courts and customs of pre-conquest England; of feudal tenure and service that secured to them the personal co-operation in war and politics of the leading men; and of royal official administration centred in their own court and household.

In the period 1087–1154 all three bases of power were to be tested. William II was confronted on his accession with a feudal revolt, and he appealed to the English element among his subjects to back him up, calling them '*his* Englishmen,' and threatening those who held back with the disgraceful native epithet of *Nithing*—good-for-nothing; and it worked. With equal success he used the feudal procedure in his court after the revolt to deal with the bishop of Durham, calling on his peers, the lay barons, to give judgment on him. He was able, moreover, to count on their financial backing when his elder brother, the crusader Robert, offered him Normandy as security for a substantial loan.

His younger brother, Henry I, who succeeded him after twelve years, leaned more heavily upon the official element in the monarchy, but he also exploited the native tradition to the full. Unlike the Conqueror's older sons he had been born in England, and his English subjects preferred him to Robert. He re-enforced William I's order that shire and hundred courts should be held as in Edward's day, ordering the sheriffs to observe local custom and not manipulate time and place to suit their own convenience.

It was in his reign that two elaborate statements of the law and custom of England were written down, as some attempt to define the 'laws of the Confessor' that Henry and his father had sworn to observe. More striking to the imagination was his marriage to a lady of the old royal house, the daughter of St. Margaret of Scotland and the great-great-granddaughter of Ethelred II. His more snobbish vassals nicknamed the king and queen Godric and Godgifu, and the gesture has been associated with a revival of the English tongue for courtly and literate use; if the son of Edith and Henry had ever reigned, the history of English literature might have been different.

But the main objection that his barons had to bring against Henry was not his kindliness to English custom, but his failure to observe the feudal code. At his coronation he had issued a charter in which the oath to act justly was expanded into specific promises to recognize certain rights of his vassals, both ecclesiastical and lay, and not to abuse his position as overlord by extorting excessive payments from them. These promises Henry broke; he exacted heavier occasional dues from his vassals than feudal custom sanctioned, and he invaded their right to do justice on their own men, rights which involved profit as well as prestige.

These exactions are to be associated with the changes introduced by Henry and his able official, Roger, Bishop of Salisbury. It is entirely characteristic of the genius of English government that the first department in which important innovations were made after the Norman Conquest was the financial. We may or may not be 'a nation of shopkeepers,' but our governmental advance has again and again been incidental to some new device for exploiting the national wealth, and our constitutional struggles, from Magna Carta to the Parliament Act, have centred in financial issues.

When Henry, looking for talent where he could find it, 'raised men of ignoble descent from the dust,' he put his finances in the hands of men familiar with the latest and most up-to-date methods of calculation, who imported from Sicily or, maybe, northern France the Arabic device of the abacus or chessboard which gave its name to the Exchequer. The new name stands for an overhaul of the Anglo-Saxon system by which the accounts of the local agents of the crown were checked. It marks the first emergence of a specialized department of the king's court, and the beginning of that differentiation of function which was to produce an expert civil service with its own traditions and its own *esprit de corps*.

The 'laws of the Exchequer' were ultimately to become almost as effective a limitation of the caprices of arbitrary power as the common law of a later generation, but in the days of Henry I they represented a great extension of the effective powers of the crown, serving not only to control the corrupt or lawless sheriff by bringing him to book rapidly and unequivocally, but also to strengthen the king's hand against his feudal magnates. The earliest surviving Exchequer record, belonging to the year 1130, shows Henry exacting extortionate fines from his barons and interfering constantly between them and their vassals. By feudal law, his lord's court should be the tribunal where a man sought justice in all cases affecting his holding or his dealings with fellow-tenants; the fief held of the king by a baron, his 'honour,' was a community of men linked with each other and their lord by his court. Henry, as royal guardian of justice, was inviting men to apply to him rather than to their lords, and either putting pressure on a baron to take action, 'lest I be troubled with further complaints,' or dealing with the case by his own officials, and thus depriving the lord of the profits of justice. In the long run this was to be in the national interest, but in 1130 it was a violation of the accepted code, and it provoked the resentment of just those men whose loyal co-operation was indispensable to Henry both at home and abroad.

He was his father's son both in his obstinate determination to have his own way and in his love for efficiency and order. In his adoption of modern methods, and in his employment of able men regardless of their origins, he belonged to the younger generation, and looked towards that awakening of initiative and genius which we are accustomed to call the Twelfth Century Renaissance. He had had public opinion on his side when in 1102 he suppressed the revolt of his lawless vassal Robert of Bellême; in his later years he defied it, and his final attempt to coerce his barons was fatal both to his own plans and to the peace and prosperity of England.

His son William had been drowned on the tragic pleasure voyage of the *White Ship* in 1120, and a hastily wedded second wife was childless. Both in theory and in practice the consent of the leading men of the realm was the only valid title to the throne, as had been proved in 1066, 1087, and 1100. In 1120 the choice lay between his brother's son William, his sister's son Stephen of Blois, and his daughter Maud, the childless widow of the Emperor Henry V.

Henry induced his barons to accept Maud as his prospective heir in 1127, undertaking that she should not be remarried without their approval, and then married her to Geoffrey of Anjou, his French neighbour, without consulting more than one or two of his magnates. It was an evil precedent. The very basis of feudal society was the sanctity of the plighted word, and the lord of the realm, in tricking his baronage, had shaken the foundations of political life. Twice more the baronage were induced to pledge their support to Maud, the last time in association with her infant son, but when Henry I died suddenly in 1135, Maud and her husband were rejected as 'aliens' by the barons of England, including Stephen, who felt free to break an oath originally obtained on false pretences.

Stephen had the advantage of being on the spot, but the greater advantage of coming in on the wave of a feudal reaction provoked by Henry I's ruthless efficiency and violation of the gentleman's agreement with his barons. To make a shaky position surer, he entered into a series of ill-considered bargains, making lavish promises to the senior earl, Maud's half-brother, Robert of Gloucester, to the citizens of London, to the Church, and to the people at large in return for their support, and bestowed earldoms and castles on his supporters. It soon became clear that he would not be able to honour his obligations, and when he brought in hired troops from overseas and quarrelled with Roger of Salisbury and his clerical kinsmen, the officials who controlled justice and finance, he not only weakened the system on which he depended, but antagonized the Church.

The dissatisfied barons took up arms; Maud came over from Anjou to try her chances, and on his first serious reverse the clergy, led by the Papal Legate, who had secured his acceptance six years earlier, deposed him in a solemn council in 1141. God had given judgment against him in battle, and in his place they elected as Lady of England and Normandy 'the daughter of the peaceful, the glorious, the wealthy, the excellent king, incomparable in our times.'

For the next twelve years, civil war was endemic in England. Neither Stephen nor Maud had effective control of England; both granted earldoms and liberties lavishly to gain support. With no effective power at the centre, the country had to run itself, and the small man suffered. A grant of land to a monastery about the year 1150 provides: 'If the war be so great that we cannot keep our animals safe, the monks shall keep them with theirs without payment. If I or my wife or my son should happen to be taken prisoner, the monks shall send one of their brethren to help us by mediation.'

A story told to the king's justices in Warwickshire some seventy years later gives us a notion of what the anarchy meant to those of the knightly class. 'In the wars of King Stephen there was a certain honest, wandering knight called Warin of Walecote, and as he journeyed and fought he came at length to the house of Robert of Shuckburgh, who had a daughter called Isabel, and he fell in love with her and asked her father to give her to him, but both Robert and his son William refused. But William, who was also a knight, went out to the wars and was killed; and Warin, hearing of this, came with an armed band and carried off Isabel against her father's will and kept her for a long time.

'But at last King Stephen died and the peace of King Henry was proclaimed, and Warin fell into poverty because he could no longer rob as he used to do; yet he could not abstain from robbery, and went robbing far and wide. And King Henry, hearing complaints of him, ordered him to be seized; and they went out after him and took him hiding in a swamp, and he was brought before the king, who, wishing to make an example of him, that others might keep the peace, commanded him to be put in the pillory, and there he died. And Isabel returned to her father's house with her child; and her father took her back because she had gone against her will, and later she married and had another son.'

The mounted warrior and the castle, reserved for royal use under the first three Norman kings, had, in fact, escaped from the control of the crown and become any man's tools. The gloomy eloquence with which the Peterborough monk concludes the chronicle continued since Alfred's days, is a complete condemnation of the feudal baron and all his works. But it would be as wrong to identify the monsters, who 'built castles and filled them with devils who tortured men,' with the average feudatory as it would be to identify a London police station with the local headquarters of the Gestapo; and the fenland chronicler who wrote, scourged by the ravages of Geoffrey de Mandeville, 'Christ slept, and his saints,' was ignoring the advances in canon law, monasticism, and good learning that were taking place in these years under Henry of Winchester, Archbishop Theobald, and the Cistercians.[1]

It may be said with justice that the moral of Stephen's reign is that 'feudalism is not enough.' Without the effective force of a non-feudal administrative system behind it to make it work, the moral obligation of plighted faith was not strong enough to hold society together. The activity of the king's court was needed to counter the centrifugal tendencies that drove each locality back on its own resources and produced disintegration.

But the nineteen winters during which England suffered for her sins produced evidence to the credit of feudalism also; the anarchy evoked a constructive response. The feudal lords who had for seventy years been doing rough justice in their courts for their tenants, and had with them built up a fair working system of landholders' rights, had successors ready to take responsibility, who helped in their own way to fill the vacuum created by the failure of the monarchy.

By mutual arrangements they tried to minimize the horrors of civil war; great earls made treaties limiting the armaments they would use against each other if a raid became inevitable. Nor did the communal courts cease to function. In 1150 an

[1]See below, pp. 129 ff.

old gentleman of East Anglia told a shire court at Norwich that he had been attending shire and hundred courts, man and boy, for fifty years, and though he looked back regretfully to the days of good King Henry, when peace and justice flourished, he was able to assert that the rights of St. Edmund's Abbey had always been respected so long as he could remember. In spite of the attack upon its key men in 1139, the Exchequer had continued to hold sessions for scrutinizing the sheriffs' accounts. The strong direction from the centre had lapsed, but there was no complete breakdown of governmental machinery, and Stephen's successor was able to take up the ruler's task, in the secular sphere at least, where Henry I had laid it down, the wiser for Henry's mistakes.

That successor was not Stephen's son, but Maud's. Henry, duke of Normandy and count of Anjou since 1151, had added Poitou and Aquitaine to his dominions by his marriage in 1152 to Eleanor of Aquitaine, the ex-wife of the king of France, and in 1153, at the age of twenty, he came over to England prepared to fight for it. But Stephen lost heart on the death of his eldest son a few months later. Before the end of the year the rivals had agreed to a settlement whereby Henry was to succeed Stephen in England, Stephen's children being secured his French lands. The castles built without royal permission were to be destroyed—1,100 of them; lands seized by violence were to be returned to their lawful owners; agriculture was to be restored, the coinage standardized, the armed forces disbanded. 'The knights were to turn their swords into ploughshares and their spears into pruning-hooks.' Nine months later Stephen died and the peace of King Henry was proclaimed.

CHAPTER VII

HENRY II AND THE COMMON LAW

IF the Norman Conquest can fairly be called the most important event in English history, it may equally well be maintained that Henry II was the king whose actions influenced the development of our institutions more than any ruler of England before or since. He laid the foundations of our common law system, and it is the continuing influence of our common law that has given us our limited monarchy, that characteristically English solution of the problem of how to reconcile liberty with order.

The young man who became king of England in 1154 was the child of his age, and it was a great age. Europe, battered and broken by the three-fold attack of Viking, Magyar, and Moslem in the ninth century, had been laboriously rebuilding her life, reconstructing her society, reviving her trade, reforming her religion up to the point when she had sufficient security to accumulate wealth and sufficient wealth to afford non-productive artistic and intellectual activity.

The tenth and eleventh centuries had seen the creation of islands of culture and industry in the new towns and monasteries; now in the twelfth it was as if men had suddenly realized their resources, and the fountains were opened for an outflow of human energy, self-confident, enterprising, exhilarated by the glimpse of new possibilities. In the schools of Italy and northern France scholars drew to themselves crowds of eager listeners; men pursued knowledge not only in the Greek and Latin authors preserved by students like Alcuin, but also in the writings of alien contemporaries, Arab doctors and mathematicians, Hebrew rabbis, and Byzantine clerks.

England had felt the stir of this awakening even under Stephen. The new writers on canon law were being studied in the new religious houses. Archbishop Theobald's household was a centre of learning and culture, and one of his guests, the Italian scholar, Vacarius, lectured on Roman Law to the students of Oxford. And in the second half of the twelfth century England's scholars and writers could hold their own with those of any country of northern Europe.

In the philosophical treatises and the correspondence of John of Salisbury, in the memoirs of Walter Map and Giraldus Cambrensis, in the biographies of Thomas Becket and Hugh of Lincoln, in the unique accounts of their offices written by the judge, Ranulf Glanvill, and the treasurer, Richard Fitz Neal, in the magnificent chronicles of William of Malmesbury, William of Newburgh, Benedict of Peterborough, Roger Howden, and many others, we have a volume of literature that reflects the vivid and many-sided life of the times. Geoffrey of Monmouth's *History of the Britons* was the twelfth-century equivalent of a best-seller, despised by good classicists and sound historians, but read all over western Europe, and a parent of a vast progeny of Arthurian stories and poems.

With the possible exception of John of Salisbury, the schools of England, forerunners of the universities of the next generation, did not produce scholastic philosophers who could rank with those of northern France, but in the application of the new arts and sciences to practical purposes England led western Europe. France and Germany had nothing to show to equal Glanvill's book on the Laws of England. Henry II himself, no less than civil servants, lawyers, historians, and memoir writers of his court, reflected this characteristically English practical bent.

It was in England that Henry had received his training as a boy. He had had what was the equivalent for a young feudal noble of those days of a first-class public-school education at Bristol Castle, in the household of his uncle Robert, earl of Gloucester, the supporter by turns of Stephen and Maud.

Henry was the descendant not only of Alfred the Great, but of that count of Anjou who said, 'A king without letters is a crowned ass,' and though the arts of warfare had not been left out of his education, the political and military matters in which he had been actively concerned from the age of sixteen never prevented his taking a lively interest in the techniques of scholarship and science. One of the brilliant writers of his court wrote to a friend in Sicily: 'Your king is a good scholar, but ours is far better; with him there is school every day, constant conversation of the best scholars and discussion of questions.' 'He knew all the languages from Gaul to the Jordan,' said another. Twenty books still extant were dedicated to him, including a *Treatise on the Astrolabe*, a *Life of Edward the Confessor*, a *History of France*, written in verse, a work on falconry, and *The Dialogue of the Exchequer*.

His intense intellectual curiosity was equalled by his physical energy. He refused to sit down for the transaction of business; he was great at hunting and hawking. He kept his courtiers on the run by his unpredictable activities: 'O Lord God, turn the heart of this king that he may know himself to be but man!' He was a mass of contradictions, generous, thrifty, untidy, orderly, unscrupulous, just, passionate, restrained; a good master who chose his servants well, yet liked to have a finger in every pie. To some of his contemporaries his energy seemed literally fiendish, inherited from a demon ancestress.

But diplomacy as well as driving force was needed for Henry's task in 1154. Stephen's reign had shown up the defects of feudalism pure and simple, but it did not prove that feudalism was the natural enemy of kingship. The robber baron is no more the typical tenant of the twelfth century than the much-divorced Hollywood star is the typical married woman of the twentieth. If the king needed his barons' co-operation in war and in government, and depended on feudal dues to make up his revenue, the baron's interests equally called for an authority that would protect his property and uphold his rights over other men.

The twelfth century was an age of economic expansion both in town and country. With lands to develop by judicious cultivation and colonization, with mercantile centres that might be both convenient and profitable under his patronage, the baron was no less ready than the smaller man to welcome the re-establishment of law and order. It is significant that when nineteen years later Henry's French vassals rose against him, instigated by his French overlord and his discontented sons, only a few English magnates joined them. 'If Henry's sons expected a glad response in England to the call of anarchy, they were disillusioned.'

Henry II set out to supply what the times demanded. Secure possession of property, and a ready means of establishing a title to land—these were the commodities that he offered the freeholders of England. His judges protected the man in possession by refusing to recognize the legality of self-help, and for establishing the facts of the case, the king put at his subjects' disposal machinery available hitherto only as a special favour at a high price, the use of a jury of neighbours in place of the judicial duel. In the king's court the man whose title was questioned could obtain a judgment far more rapidly than in the feudal or communal courts, where the long-drawn-out ritual of customary procedure had to be followed. Further, the litigant could be sure that execution would follow a judgment, because the king had means of enforcement that no one else could command. If he preferred the older procedure, he could apply to the king's Chancery for a writ commanding his lord to hear the case in his own court.

For the benefit of the smaller freeholders who could not afford long journeys to the king's court, royal judges visited the shires regularly to hear cases by the new procedure. As these judges came from the king's court and returned to it, the rules they applied in their conduct of cases were the same all over England, and all future developments in legal process were to be common to all England. Henry did not set out to make new laws; he only offered new procedures, but in applying the new principles and new procedures his judges were setting up precedents which were the starting-point of the whole body of later common law.

The rights the king chose to protect, not created by him, but protected by him, came to be associated for all men with the procedures he offered; trial by jury, the 'benefit graciously bestowed' by Henry on his subjects, was to become one of an Englishman's most proudly cherished rights. By these innovations Henry had given every landholder, great and small, an interest in royal authority; he had used his power to safeguard the ancient rights of his subjects; and he had linked together communal custom and royal justice by sending his judges to the shire courts and making local knowledge the determining proof.

Royal justice became so popular that the Exchequer had to devise new methods of entering up judicial payments; more judges had to be appointed; and in the following century the central court had to be sub-divided into three branches. The business done in the feudal courts dwindled rapidly; the barons found the new processes so useful for their own purposes that in 1215 they made John promise to send royal justices into every shire four times a year, a promise that proved impossible of fulfilment.

Alongside this indirect attack on self-help and violence, Henry used more drastic methods. Unlicensed castles were destroyed, and for the detection and punishment of murder, robbery, and arson, the king once more called for the co-operation of local juries. The men of the vill, the hundred, and the shire were required upon oath to report suspects to the king's justices, and the local officials were to seize and guard them, building new gaols where necessary, until the royal justices came to try them. The feudal lord who did his part in catching the criminals might still punish them, if he had had the right previously; the negligent forfeited the profits of justice.

It is not only from the chroniclers that we learn this. The story stands written in the admirably kept rolls of the Exchequer and of the other sessions of the king's court, which record the activities of judges and administrators and the means by which the ever watchful king kept an eye on his own agents. Officials from the centre inspected local government in the shires; local juries were invited to report the misconduct both of sheriffs and bailiffs, and of the officials of the barons who had similar functions in their liberties.

Only in one quarter were Henry's efforts frustrated. When his judges reported to him early in his reign that certain men arrested on a charge of crime claimed exemption from the king's jurisdiction because they were clergy, he asserted this to be contrary to right and custom. In a council held at Clarendon Palace in 1164, he induced the leading clergy to put their names to a statement that, amongst various other old customs, a clerk convicted in the bishop's court ought to be handed over for punishment to lay authorities. His former chancellor and present archbishop, Thomas Becket, withdrew from this statement, upheld the privilege of the clerk to be tried, sentenced, and punished only by the ecclesiastical authorities, and appealed to Pope Alexander III for support.

Alexander, embarrassed by his supporter's assertion of a claim not yet established anywhere, but unwilling to repudiate so zealous a churchman, used his influence to secure a reconciliation, but the compromise arrived at after six years of negotiation was instantly wrecked by the pride of Becket, the temper of Henry, and the ferocious zeal of Henry's courtiers. The archbishop, just returned from exile, was murdered in his own cathedral, and it became impossible for Henry to refuse whatever terms the Pope exacted.

Those terms registered the victory of the canon law of the Catholic Church over the common law of the English monarchy. A man who could prove he was a clerk was withdrawn from royal justice, which meant that no clerk could be hanged for murder or theft. All litigants in church courts might appeal freely to the Roman curia without royal licence; which meant that the law of the English Church, as regarded both clerics and laymen, must conform to Roman standards and not to local custom. The door that William had kept shut, that had blown open under Stephen, and that Henry had tried to close, was now set wide open. Disputes as to marriages, testaments, sacrilege, perjury, elections to bishoprics, might all come before the tribunal of the Pope as the ultimate interpreter of canon law.

The penance at Becket's tomb and the subsequent agreement with Alexander III registered Henry's first great defeat, but not his last. Once again, his enemies were those of his own household. His wife and his sons turned against him, instigated and aided by the kings of France and Scotland. Henry, as we have seen, got the better of the great coalition of 1173, in which his three elder sons were involved. But for the last eight years of his reign, Richard, backed by the French king, was constantly at war with his father in France, and finally John, his youngest son, also turned against him.

The patron of the arts, the founder of the common law, the lord of more than half France, whose daughters were married to dukes and kings from Bavaria to Castile, died heartbroken at the destruction of his Angevin birthplace by his enemies, and the desertion of his youngest and most beloved son. 'Shame, shame on a conquered king!' is an ironic recessional for a ruler with so august a record.

CHAPTER VIII

THE BARONIAL REACTION: RUNNYMEDE AND EVESHAM

I

1189–1216

HENRY II might write himself down a failure, but the work that he had done lived after him. Richard, his successor, half troubadour, half crusader, spent barely six months of his ten years of kingship in England. But the royal government could now function without a king. There was no return to the anarchy of Stephen's reign. Richard's absences and preoccupations, however, subjected the government and people of England to new strains, the reaction to which was highly significant.

The demand for ready money, first for crusading expenses, then to provide Richard's ransom, and, after his return, to finance his wars in France, was responsible in the first place for new forms of taxation that tapped industrial as well as agrarian wealth, and also led to the sale of chartered liberties to the boroughs on a scale that Richard's father would never have sanctioned. The king's absence led to the appointment of officials to see to the keeping of the peace—a species of special constable with powers of discretionary arrest, in whom have been recognized the far-off ancestors of the J.P.; and finally, produced a large scale political crisis in 1191, when Longchamps, the tactless and aggressive deputy appointed by Richard, exceeded his powers, and the leading barons took common action with the citizens of London to vindicate the lawful customs of the realm.

What might have been a mere partisan gesture gained significance by the formal action of the magnates; judicial sentence was passed by the king's court in his absence, and the same body, acting without the king, assumed the responsibilities of

·government until Richard's return. John's designs on the throne had been defeated before his brother returned to exact the due penalties from his treacherous brother.

The events of 1191 were the first indication that the baronage could act as a body and were prepared to appeal to the forms and customs of the law against the king's officials. No baron or freeman, they declared, ought to be dispossessed without lawful trial. Hubert Walter, Longchamps' successor, had been trained in the art and practice of government by Henry II's great lawyers; his administration both of finance and of justice was fertile in effective devices; and when John succeeded his far from vindictive brother in 1199, the monarchy was stronger than it had ever been.

If the moral of Richard's reign might seem to be that the personal factor counted for little in English government, the reign of John was to prove the contrary. To the absentee knight-errant, Provençal rather than English in his character and tastes, succeeded a man who 'probably knew England better than any other ruler prior to Edward VII.' Of his father's four sons, he was the one reared in England; his patron saint was Wulfstan of Worcester, who, within ten years of the Norman Conquest, had been the only Englishman still holding a bishopric in his native land. The King is said to have told the Roman cardinals the story of how William the Conqueror, attempting to oust the bishop because he could speak no French, had been frustrated by the miraculous intervention of another English saint, Edward the Confessor, whose throne and whose ecclesiastical prerogatives he, John, inherited. But however much he might play the Anglophile, the demon of the Angevins was in his blood no less than in his father's and brother's.

Brilliant, restless, varying in mood from violence to lethargy, sensuous, clever, sarcastic, but cruel and treacherous, John was completely unreliable. The magnificent machine of administration devised by his father and perfected by Hubert Walter could become, under such a man, as deadly and detestable as Victor Hugo's cannon when it broke loose on the decks of the corvette.

John's cleverness was of the individualistic and irresponsible type that defies not only convention but common humanity, not only the rule of law but the rules of the game. He had great assets; the fidelity of royal servants and the loyalty of feudal barons; he could, and did, appeal successfully to the community of the realm when danger from outside threatened; he could, as it proved when the pinch came, count on the backing of a large proportion of the clergy. But he resented the restriction imposed on him by the service of faithful officials, and is reported to have rejoiced shamelessly at the death of his justiciar Geoffrey Fitzpeter.

His violations of the code of feudal conduct between overlord and vassals finally lost him the support of the majority of his barons; the military ineptitude, which earned him the byname of 'Soft-sword,' proved him unable to discharge the first duty of a medieval king to his subjects, and lost him both his paternal dominions in Normandy and Anjou, and the prestige won by his father and brother, whilst in defying the authority of the Pope he challenged a power that had advanced both morally and administratively far beyond the stage at which his father had had to yield to it.

He had against him the constructive forces of a law-making age—the administrative ability of the French king, his former friend, Philip Augustus; the majestic tradition of the canon law embodied in the greatest of the Popes, Innocent III; and the established customs of English law and kingship, formulated for reluctant rebels by the statesman archbishop, Stephen Langton.

The record evidence of the mounting efficiency of governmental machinery in law and, above all, finance is unmistakable under John. The king's hand lay heavily on his subjects; but extortionate taxation would not alone have produced revolt. It was the seizure of Normandy by his French overlord in 1204, and John's failure to recover it in subsequent campaigns, that laid him open to the attacks of a baronage with many private as well as public grievances.

Nor did the danger from France end with the loss of Normandy. Hubert Walter's death in 1205 meant not only the removal of John's ablest servant, but a vacancy in the See of Canterbury. A disputed election followed; and Innocent III, with whom, under canon law, the decision rested, turned down both John's candidate and his rival, and indicated to the electors an English scholar of some forty-five years, Stephen Langton, whose lectures in the schools of Paris had established his fame with contemporaries and have given posterity evidence of his approach to the political problems of his own country. They reflect his belief in the rule of law; the all-transcending law of nature, which he saw, as Wordsworth saw it, divinely governing the actions of men; and the law of the community which he saw, as Burke saw it, authorized by custom and commonsense and formulated by authority. The arbitrary command of despotism, the conception that might is right, he utterly condemned. Justice and equity were not remote abstractions; through law they became practicable. 'Ought a subject to obey a wrongful command of the ruler? Not if it proceeds from the ruler's arbitrary will; but if it expresses the declared judgment of his court, yes, because it is not for a private person to go behind the decision of the duly constituted authority.'

But not for seven years was the archbishop's statesmanship to be evoked. John refused to accept Stephen, and ejected those bishops who recognized his authority. One diplomatic exchange after another proved abortive. The Pope prohibited all church services by an interdict; John simply seized the lands of the Church. Then John himself was excommunicated. The English public, whose recognition of the Pope's spiritual authority alone made such censures effective, had by 1212 reached a state when the wildest rumours were believed. The Welsh were in revolt; Philip Augustus was preparing to invade England, and Innocent's ultimatum of February 1213 included a scarcely veiled threat to release John's subjects from their allegiance.

John was not prepared to risk simultaneous rebellion and invasion; in May 1213 he submitted and became the Pope's vassal, securing the privileges of a vowed crusader. The tables were turned, and not only for Philip Augustus. The archbishop who had stood up for Papal rights, and the barons who had loyally supported the king throughout the interdict were confronted with a new alliance of king and Pope. Relying on Innocent's support, John was prepared to defy both feudal custom and the oath which Stephen Langton had exacted from him when he was absolved in 1213; an oath 'to restore the good laws of his predecessors, especially of St. Edward, and to do justice to all men according to the judgments of his court.'

Baronial resentment at John's high-handed conduct was given a constructive form by the archbishop, who reminded the malcontents of Henry I's coronation charter of 1100 defining the rights he had sworn to observe. By similar means, he suggested, they might secure the restoration of the liberties 'long lost' under John. When, in 1214, John returned to England, after the complete failure of his attempt to restore his military fortunes in France, he was confronted by a united front of archbishop and barons with a constructive programme.

They requested him to fulfil the oath that he had sworn at his absolution; and as to what the good laws and customs of the realm were, they were preparing a statement that he would be asked to accept and endorse, in the drafting of which they had certainly had expert legal assistance. It soon became clear that only under compulsion would John give such a pledge. Both sides prepared for war, the opposition barons giving notice in due feudal form of their 'defiance' or repudiation of fealty.

John, having vainly tried to detach the clergy by granting them a separate charter, found that the Exchequer could not provide him with funds, that the city of London and the home counties were on the side of the barons, and that not only his archbishop, but those moderate and loyal older barons who were at his own side, advised his acceptance of the petition, in spite of the final coercive clause appointing a committee of twenty-five barons to enforce fulfilment of his undertakings. A week's conference on the bank of the Thames below Windsor transformed the petition into a charter, sealed with the great seal, and carried down to the shires that all men might know of it.

The drama of Runnymede can easily mislead us as to the significance of Magna Carta. It was a feudal document, applying the feudal principle of contract, exacted by vassals from a lord who had failed to fulfil his duty to them. But it was no less an application of the ancient tradition embodied in the coronation oath, that the ruler of England was bound to observe the established customs of the land which made him king. These ancient customs in shire and hundred and township were older than feudalism, and belonged to all free men, and John was made to promise that he would appoint men who knew and would observe them to rule in the shires. Even more noteworthy was the fact that those who drafted the charter followed the archbishop in regarding the king's own court as a trustworthy guardian of the law; they asked for feudal judgment by a man's peers, but in demanding the law of the land they also asked for frequent visitations of the shires by royal justices, and for the prisoner's right to have a jury without payment of a fee.

In the short run, however, Magna Carta was the banner of insurrection. Innocent absolved John from his promises, excommunicated the barons, and suspended Stephen Langton for his refusal to condemn them. There was a brief period of attempted co-operation; but twelve weeks after the sealing of the charter war had begun. All the more moderate barons rallied to John's side. He had trained mercenaries, and his own capricious military brilliance was at last displayed in full. Castle after castle fell to his arms, and before the end of 1215 the rebels saw nothing for it but to call in foreign aid. Louis, the son of Philip Augustus, landed in Kent in May 1216. When John died, five months later, it seemed as if a deadlock had been reached.

But once again the feudal ruling class was to give evidence of its growing political maturity. The barons had used legal process to oust an autocrat in 1191, they had appealed to law in 1214 before resorting to force. Now, in 1216, John's faithful adherents, led by the valiant old Earl Marshal, whose memories went back to the days of Stephen, renewed the alliance of the monarchy and the law which Henry II had established. In the name of John's young son, Henry III, they reissued the Great Charter, purged of its most controversial clauses, and so stole the thunder of the young hotheads who had already alienated sympathy by inviting French aid.

Archbishop Stephen was at Rome, making his peace with the Pope; the rebels cut their losses and came to terms. Within a year of John's death Louis had gone home to France.

II
1216–1272

Twice in the long reign of John's son the English baronage took common action against their king. With a good working conscience, with warm family affections, and with a genuine devotion to religion and the Papacy, Henry III yet had his share of the Angevin legacy, his father's moodiness and unreliability no less than his biting tongue. He was nine years old when his father died, and when he emerged from the minority, during which the functions of government had been exercised by a group of older barons helped by the papal legate, he had much to learn.

After dismissing his father's faithful servant Hubert de Burgh, he turned to the experts of the civil service, mostly foreigners, and tried his hand at autocracy for a short spell when he was twenty-five years old. He learned his lesson, not only from the opposition of the saintly archbishop who had succeeded Stephen, and from his barons' formal renunciation of fealty and threat of deposition, but from the dire results of his own actions when a leading earl was assassinated in his name. For good or for ill, an English king could not dispense with the goodwill and co-operation of his barons. Henry III, like his father, had to recognize and accept the limitations formulated in the Great Charter, now part of the law of the land enforced in the courts.

For thirty-five years, before the storm broke in 1258, the more or less uneasy partnership of king and barons endured. But the recurrent grumblings of either party, all too vividly depicted by the St. Albans monk, Matthew Paris, should not be allowed to drown the full triumphant theme of thirteenth-century England—the high middle ages of our history.

It is the period of those royal justices whose wisdom and

sanity laid down the precedents of our legal system. A protest
by six of them in 1218 against a government directive strikes an
independent note re-echoed by generations of English judges.
'You appointed us to this task for the peace of the lord
King and the Kingdom, to do justice to poor as well as rich,
and it would not befit his honour or ours that we should do
anything contrary to the custom of the realm.' Their work
bore fruit in the great book written by one of their number,
Bracton of Devonshire, which declared English customary law
well worthy to stand beside the written law of Rome, and
English kingship to be based on the law framed in the king's
court and promulgated by himself; for 'without law a king
is a tyrant.'

It is the period when agricultural and industrial progress
is multiplying the population in town and country; when
fresh land is being brought under the plough, and new methods
in husbandry are being expounded in writing; when the flocks
of sheep are multiplying on the Yorkshire and Lincolnshire
wolds, on the hills of Shropshire and Gloucestershire, on the
estates of the Cistercian abbeys and of the bishops of Winchester
and Ely; when in the towns the craftsmen are beginning to
organize themselves in gilds to maintain the level both in
quality and in price of their handiwork; when the civic pride
of the burgesses is borrowing from France the title and office
of mayor as the embodiment of conscious community, and the
government is delegating to him and his bailiffs wider administrative responsibilities by means of the charters which the
growing wealth of the towns enables them to purchase.

It is the period when England is becoming articulate, with
written records of courts, manuals of husbandry, popular
political ballads, love lyrics in the vernacular, and our first
round, 'Sumer is icumen in,' is noted in words and music.
The great men have left the shire court, and the country
gentlemen are running it, and holding their own successfully
against the king's sheriff if he tries to 'drive' them. 'This is
the custom of our shire, and the king has promised it us in
the great charter.'

The communities of shire, hundred, and vill, employed by

the Norman and Angevin kings for the keeping of the king's peace and the exercise of the king's justice, are now being used to assess the king's taxes. The social and political consciousness of the knightly class is awakening, stimulated by such activities. Summoned to the king's court in the twelfth century to report on proceedings in the shire, their representatives are now coming there to report what the shire can contribute to the king's financial needs. Soon the knights and burgesses will be called on, both by barons in opposition and by Henry himself, to take sides in the dispute as to how the realm should be governed, for it is they who supply the tools of government and the sinews of war. The barons may call themselves the community of the realm, but the communities of shire, borough, and vill represent the resources that can turn the scale in the struggle.

It is the age of the coming of the friars and of the setting up of numerous humble houses of Franciscans, Dominicans, and Poor Clares.[1] It is the age when the schools of Oxford and Cambridge are claiming the title of Universities, and great men like Grosseteste and Roger Bacon are making those schools famous. It is an age of pilgrimages, notably to St. Thomas's Shrine at Canterbury, but also to Lincoln, St. Albans, Durham, Ely, Rochester, Worcester, and Winchester, and it is to the offerings of pilgrims, no less than to the devotion of kings or bishops, that we owe the architectural glories of this reign, when English builders were realizing the possibilities of the pointed arch and the vaulted roof, and the Romanesque splendours of Durham and Gloucester and Christ Church were being succeeded by the shafted and soaring vistas of the new style. The new cathedral at Salisbury was built between 1220 and 1258. The west fronts of Wells and Peterborough, the presbyteries of Ely and Worcester, the great transepts of York and Durham and Rochester, the chapter houses of Chester and Lincoln and Lichfield, were all rising, whilst at Westminster Henry III was seeking to rival the achievements of his brother-in-law of France, and running into debt as he sought to make the Abbey Church a fitting shrine for the relics of his patron, Edward the Confessor, after whom he had named his eldest son.

[1] See below, pp. 131 f.

It was his second son, Edmund, named after the East Anglian martyr, who was the innocent cause of the impasse which put Henry at the mercy of his barons. The Popes had for a long time tried to draw upon English wealth to finance their wars with the Hohenstaufen; now, in 1255, Alexander IV offered Henry the crown of Sicily for his son in return for a large sum. Henry could not bear to refuse the offer, but the money was not forthcoming, and in 1257, threatened with excommunication for failure to pay up, he was forced to throw himself on the mercy of his barons.

In the Easter parliament of 1258, after discussions lasting for a month, Henry and his son Edward agreed to the setting up of a joint committee of royal and baronial nominees to set in order the state of the realm, and promised on oath to accept their recommendations; in return the barons undertook to settle the king's financial difficulties. In the parliament held at Midsummer 1258 at Oxford the committee began its work, and the constitutional experiment of joint government by king and barons was fairly launched by August.

The experiment cannot be said to have finally broken down until January 1264, when King Louis of France, asked to adjudicate on the provisions made for the government of the realm at Oxford, went beyond his commission and declared them altogether null and void, and the baronial opposition appealed from his arbitrament to that of arms. Even before that date both parties had charged the other with breach of faith.

Personal rivalries and misunderstandings had further complicated the issue. It was not a simple cleavage between the king and his kinsmen on the one hand and the barons on the other. Simon de Montfort, the ardent, idealistic Frenchman, who ultimately became sole leader of the opposition, was Henry's brother-in-law. At one point (1259–60) even the Lord Edward, the heir to the throne, had wavered. The king's brother, Richard of Cornwall, whose financial and diplomatic skill might have averted the crisis if Henry had taken his advice, held aloof for a while, but finally espoused his cause unequivocally. Henry's Poitevin half-brothers were

completely intransigent, and greatly strengthened anti-alien
sentiment in the reforming party. Within that party the
leaders, notably Richard of Clare and Simon de Montfort,
quarrelled with each other; the clergy were divided, some
being ardently baronial, some royalist, and some, like the
queen's uncle, Archbishop Boniface of Canterbury, neutral.
Many friars, though owing the king many debts of gratitude,
were passionate supporters of Simon de Montfort. The
younger generation, like Gilbert of Clare and Henry, the
son of Richard of Cornwall, took sides against their parents,
the greater burgesses were opposed by the lesser, and the
lords of the Welsh Marches played a lone hand, taking either
side in turn as their interests dictated.

The battle of Lewes (1264) which left the king, his son, and
his brother prisoners in the hands of the baronial opposition,
led to Simon de Montfort's brief dictatorship, ended by his
defeat and death at Evesham fifteen months later at the hands of
Edward and the Marcher lords, including Gilbert of Clare.
It took two more years for the King's party to come
to terms with the last of the rebels at Kenilworth, Axholme,
and Ely. Defection, death, forfeiture, and banishment had
broken up the baronial opposition, and the final settlement
declared that Henry should have his royal powers un-
abridged as before the days of the Parliament of Oxford.
In particular, the claim of the barons, constantly reiterated
ever since Henry's coming of age, and made good in practice
from 1258 to 1261, to have a say in the appointment of the great
officials, the justiciar, the treasurer, and the chancellor, was
expressly denied.

To the royal defeat at Runnymede had succeeded the far
more shattering defeat, it would seem, of the barons at Evesham
and Kenilworth. But for all this, the eggs could not be un-
scrambled and the effects of the experiment were to be lasting.

In the first place, the definite grievances of the barons put
forward at Oxford, as to defects in the law and the administration, had produced legislative reforms, drafted by trained legists,
which had been solemnly proclaimed in 1259, and were
re-issued with amendments and additions in 1267 as the

Statute of Marlborough, part of the permanent law of the land. This was a solid and lasting achievement.

In the second place, the barons had proved their sense of responsibility and their practical capacity by carrying on for two and a half years, from 1258 to 1261, the work of directing administration and policy, both domestic and foreign. Henry had accused them of being helpless amateurs, but they had, in fact, appointed the justiciar, the treasurer, and the chancellor and, until he began working against them, the financial and judicial administration had proceeded smoothly. Of more permanent significance was the emergence of the local communities as factors in the political situation. The country gentlemen, who until the middle of the century had been left to run the shires, had already been invited to approve taxation through their representatives before the king's council in 1254. From 1258 onwards they were constantly invited to take a hand in the new reforms. They were expected to hear complaints in the shire court and carry them to the king's baronial council at Westminster; to report to their shires what was being done at Westminster, taking back with them the king's proclamation, written in English for their benefit. They were even authorized to choose one of themselves to be sheriff. In 1261 they were summoned by Henry to have the political situation explained to them.

They, like the great men at the top, had found themselves compelled to take sides; would they pay their dues to the king's sheriff or the barons' sheriff? Would they, when it came to fighting, follow the banner of this or that lord? So it was not a startling innovation when Simon de Montfort, during his brief dictatorship, summoned them to the parliament of 1265, though it was a novelty for them to meet there representatives from some of the boroughs also, the earl, in need of the support of the burgesses, having summoned them also.

Lastly, one of the rules laid down by the reforming committee at Oxford was that there should be three parliaments a year. This word, *parliament*, had slipped into the political vocabulary under Henry III. It meant no more than 'conference' or 'parley'; John had held a parliament with his

barons at Runnymede; the craftsmen of London held their
parliaments on craft business; Louis IX of France and his
newly married wife used to 'hold parliament' together secretly
on a back stair of the royal palace to escape the jealous vigilance
of his mother; but by 1250 the word was coming to be used
especially for the conferences held by the king for governmental
purposes.

Departmental conferences between exchequer officials,
judges, and counsellors, and political conferences between the
king and his barons, were alike called parliaments; most
probably 'a parliament' involved many such parallel conferences and discussions. At Oxford the reformers provided
that three times a year a council of their appointment should
meet for conference with the wider circle of barons, great and
small, who were not counsellors, and in all probability such
sessions were already coming to serve as clearing houses for the
handling of petitions from all and sundry for the remedy of
private and personal grievances.

However that may be, it seems that the standard of three
parliaments a year for the discussion of public business and
the redress of grievances was permanently established in 1258.
The calendar of parliaments runs continuously from that date,
and Edward I's first act, when he took up the task of government in 1274, was to call a general parliament, to which, as his
uncle Simon had done, he summoned representatives of both
shires and boroughs; to which, as his father had done, he
submitted the drafts of his first great statutes for acceptance
and promulgation. In the short run, in fact, the most interesting
result of the troubles of Henry's reign was the effect of all
these years of experiment and mutual recrimination on his
son, the future king of England.

CHAPTER IX

THE ENGLISH JUSTINIAN
1272-1307

EDWARD I had been a strong-willed and violent young man of nineteen when the Parliament of Oxford met in 1258. In the years of conflict he had been charged by his enemies with trickery and guile, and had won more fame as a fighter than as a statesman, contributing less to the final settlement than his cousin Henry. The man of thirty-five who returned from the Crusade, during which he had suffered the loss of his father, his uncle, his two little sons, and that same much-loved cousin, had learned self-control and a due respect for the rights of others.

To the moral and social code of a Christian knight and gentleman, Edward joined a respect for and belief in law which was characteristic of the age of Bracton, Aquinas, and Alphonso the Wise of Castile, his brother-in-law. It was the good fortune of England that at the end of a century of creative activity the throne should be occupied by a man with a passion for system and definition. To the edifice built by the great legists and administrators of Henry II, and the wise and experienced judges of Henry III, Edward I's counsellors and legal experts added the coping stone in the long series of statutes promulgated in the thirty years from 1275 to 1307.

"The very scheme, mould and model, of the common law," said a seventeenth-century Chief Justice, "was set in order by this king; and so in a very great measure has continued the same in all succeeding ages to this day." A like systematization was applied to the machinery of government; local and central administration were overhauled; sheriffs, exchequer officials, household officials, found their duties and powers newly defined; a constitution was framed for the conquered countries of Wales and Scotland. The position of the lords of liberties, whether they exercised vice-regal powers in a Palatinate county, or merely acted as police magistrates on their own estates, was defined by statute and judicial inquiry.

'To all their due' might have been Edward's motto, and if he rated his own dues high, he saw his calling and his advantage in securing their dues to his subjects. Whether the idea was in the air, or whether he took it over from the barons whom he had defeated, the conception of the realm as a community was a guiding principle of Edward's government. In the society of the thirteenth century the older relationships consecrated by feudalism, those between a lord and his vassals or tenants, were coming to be less significant than those between men of the same occupation or interests—the fellow-workers in government, or craft, or trade.

The orders or estates of society, what we should to-day call the classes, were becoming more self-conscious. Edward, who had for one moment in 1259 constituted himself the champion of the knightly class, made it his aim to insist on the obligation of all such smaller groups to the whole community. Common dangers should be met by common action; none, not even the clergy, should claim exemption from the common burdens of citizenship, financial if not personal. Feudal rights were not denied, indeed, he provided machinery for their better enforcement; but the basic feudal doctrine of responsibility was given a wider application.

The clergy who benefited by the security won for them by the arms of the king and the lay barons, must bear their share in paying for it; the merchants who had royal protection must submit to increased customs duties; the communities of town and country-side, who found in the new device of royal parliaments a means of obtaining benefits for their borough or shire, must be prepared to authorize the delegates whom Edward, from time to time, ordered them to send to those same parliaments to commit them to the payment of the extra-ordinary taxes needed for the financing of an aggressive foreign policy.

There was little of the democrat about Edward I, but the common man might well feel that he counted for more in the

political community, whether as liable for duties or as entitled
to rights, than he had done at any earlier time. The representatives who were summoned to witness the trial of David
of Wales, or to lend their help to the defence of the realm,
against the evil machinations of Philip of France, 'who
proposes to wipe out the English tongue from the earth, if his
power matches his will,' might be playing a very subordinate
part in these high politics, but they were implicated in them
inevitably by the contributions they were expected to furnish
and helped to levy.

All over Europe it was financial need that was driving
princes and rulers to summon representatives of urban communities, and, in some countries, of the knightly or gentle
classes, to consult with them in matters of finance. As the pope
told St. Louis's brother in 1267, when he acquired the
kingdom of Sicily, it was easier to get money out of the barons,
clergy, and townsmen, if ways and means were first discussed
with them; 'Thus you may secure your just rights and they
their liberties.'

From the Church, also, came the legal formula, used in
Spain and Italy before Edward adopted it in England, for
ordering the communities to give *full power* to their representatives to act for them in these matters, so that the communities could not repudiate the action of the two burgesses
or the two knights they had sent to the king's parliament. To
the old pledge that linked king and vassals there was added the
new pledge linking community and representative. The
traditional consent of the royal vassals in parliament to emergency aids was reinforced by the assent of the elected knights
and burgesses, who were in a stronger position than the
middling orders of any other European country, because of
their close personal association with the powerful and politically
experienced magnate class.

In England no hard and fast barrier divided noble and
gentle, or rural and urban; in political crises, such as that of
1297, the lords fought the battle of the knights and burgesses,
and in the tussles whereby the rule was established that all
grants of money were made by the commons and agreed to

by the lords, the burgesses were glad to let the more self-assured and aggressive knightly class take the initiative on their behalf. The gentleman who had a town house as well as his manor houses in the country might serve on occasion as mayor or borough member; the successful burgess bought a country estate; and earls, knights, and burgesses alike had their common interest in the national industry of wool growing, the great and increasing source of national wealth in the thirteenth and fourteenth centuries, a treasure in which foreign and English merchants speculated and in which kings in need of ready money claimed a lion's share and thus, all unawares, forced common action on their subjects.

Edward I has been called the English Justinian, and he resembled that great emperor not only in his legislative activities. His imperialistic policy, as we should call it to-day, committed England to those military undertakings which strained his finances to breaking point, and dragged on throughout the later middle ages as a recurrent motif in English foreign relations. The claims he made were based on feudal law, and he was undoubtedly as clear that the law was on his side as any ruler of England whose self-righteousness has provoked the charge of hypocrisy from a disgusted Europe.

In Wales, as in Ireland at a later date, the conflicts of Celtic tribal law and Anglo-Norman feudal law created a complex problem. Since the Norman Conquest there had been a steady, though intermittent, penetration of the Welsh highlands and lowlands by Anglo-Norman castle builders and colonists, fighting and marrying with their Welsh neighbours. The native princes, for all their gallantry, could not make common cause, and though twice in the thirteenth century the ruler of Snowdon asserted himself as prince of all Wales, he could not maintain his overlordship without English aid. The transformation of Welsh prince into feudal baron proved impracticable, and Edward found himself driven to bring to bear on Wales the most modern techniques of warfare, diplomacy, justice, and, finally, parliamentary legislation.

The last prince of all Wales died in battle; his shifty brother suffered the death of a traitor; and English administration was superimposed on all the lands between the Dee and the Bristol Channel. Social and racial absorption was another matter, as a nationalist rising under Owen Glendower in the fifteenth century was to show; but independence was at an end, and by the time kings of Welsh blood were ruling England, it was possible to incorporate the principality in the kingdom and to summon Welsh members of parliament to Westminster.

The war in Scotland was a different story. Since the Norman Conquest the Scottish kings had been the vassals of the English kings, in much the same way as the English kings had been the vassals of the kings of France; that is, they did homage for their English lands, but not for their kingdom. Unlike the Welsh princes, they had, however, adopted a large measure of Anglo-Norman law and administrative method. Many men held lands both sides of the border and there was much inter-marriage; Edward's aunt Joan and his sister Margaret had married Scottish kings. Able kings had ruled in Scotland, but her Normans, Saxons, and Celts had not yet become a nation.

In 1290 the death of a little girl of four left Scotland with twelve claimants to the vacant throne, and in the following year the Scots accepted Edward as their overlord and as the appropriate adjudicator between the claims of the rival candidates. The award, made in accordance with the advice of a large body of assessors, on which Scots were in the majority, gave the kingdom to John Balliol, who did homage for it to Edward. Thus, when difficulties arose between the new Scottish king and his subjects, Edward had the law on his side, and could treat all who rejected his authority as traitors under feudal law.

By that law Scotland was forfeit to the overlord whose vassal had been false to him; but the attempt to incorporate Scotland with England proved once more that feudalism was not enough and called a nation into being. Two leaders were successfully eliminated, and the third, Robert Bruce, crowned king in 1306, seemed near his final defeat when Edward died on the road to Scotland in 1307, charging his son to complete his work.

The work never was completed; fourteen years after the crushing defeat of Bannockburn, Edward's grandson had to recognize the independence of Scotland; but war broke out again almost at once, and enmity between the two kingdoms was lasting. The Borders came to be a no-man's-land subject to constant raids; whilst the Scots became the close allies of France, linked with her by royal marriages, by military ventures, by language, by law, and, in the final event, by religion, for Mary Stuart's hated rival, John Knox, no less than herself, had had his education in France.

Hostility with France was no new thing. The relationship of lord and vassal between two independent rulers, difficult in itself, was further complicated by the unruliness of the English king's Gascon subjects, a problem that had baffled both Simon de Montfort and the Lord Edward during their terms of office as governors. Henry III and St. Louis, allied by marriage, by artistic taste, by religion, by political sympathies, had been official enemies, until the treaty of 1259 made the king of England once again the liegeman of the king of France, though with a holding much diminished from that of the twelfth century.

But in Louis' grandson, the unscrupulous and hard-headed Philip IV, Edward was confronted by an overlord bent on realizing French dominance and enlarging royal power, who made a sea-fight between his own and Edward's merchants in 1293 the pretext for seizing the French fiefs of the English king, and involving him in the costly military ventures that produced the parliament of 1295 and the crisis of 1297. However efficient Edward's governmental machinery was, and however much he supplemented feudal sources by hired soldiers, he could not make effective war without the military co-operation of his barons, nor, by this time, without the financial co-operation of the knights and burgesses.

The summons to the clergy, barons, and communities in 1295 to meet common dangers by common action in granting war taxes was accompanied by more dubious measures, such as the requisitioning of large quantities of wool; and two years later he found himself faced by the resistance not only of the clergy, whom Boniface VIII had forbidden to pay taxes to lay authorities, but also of the barons, who declined to go to France except in Edward's company, and who refused to consent to the tax that the king was inducing knights and merchants to approve. Only in return for a confirmation of Magna Carta, coupled with a promise to abandon the new wool duty and levy no new tax without consent, was resistance abandoned.

The clergy, released from the pope's embarrassing orders, made their contribution, and Edward carried on his French enterprise until the treaty of 1299, sealed by the marriage of himself and the betrothal of his son to French princesses, restored his Gascon fiefs to Edward. Far from ending the conflict, this left the feudal problem unsolved and was to lead to the most irreconcilable quarrel of all, when the son of Edward II and Isabel of France claimed the succession to his French uncle's throne in 1337, and launched England on the so-called Hundred Years' War, which, with its far-reaching effects on the economic resources, the political and constitutional developments, and the national outlook of both countries, was in fact only to end when the accession of Elizabeth cleared the stage for Spain to take the place of 'our sweet enemy, France.'

If these were to be the long-term consequences of Edward I's war policy, its short-term result was to make the royal power vulnerable. The royal governmental machine reached its maximum efficiency under him. The expert clerks of his household held the threads of administration in their hands, negotiated loans, provided the personnel for the great departments of state, and filled most of the seats on his council.

His judges, the pupils of Bracton's generation, did justice at Westminster and in the shires, holding inquiries both into the conduct of the local officials and into the titles of the great liberties of the king's barons and into the exercise of the privileges they enjoyed by royal grant. The barons bore their share in the government of the land, being forced to recognize that a misuse of their privileges would bring financial penalties if not forfeiture.

Edward respected their rights, as he expected them to respect his, and safeguarded many of them by statute. In his great parliaments he took counsel with them for the common good, and heard the petitions that all men were invited to lay before him there. But all through his reign he was plunging deeper and deeper into debt. The wars of his father's reign had bequeathed to him a deficit that he was never able to make good; his own Crusade and his wars in Wales, Scotland, and France increased it, and his attempts to realize some of the floating wealth of the realm involved him, as we have seen, in disputes with his subjects without materially improving the position. Like Justinian, Edward had overtasked the resources of his realm, and his successors, like Justinian's, had to pay the penalty.

CHAPTER X

THE WORKING AND WINNING
COMMUNITIES

THE reign of Edward I marks the culmination of the process of the concentration of governmental power in the monarchy. An effective challenge to its position was to be made by an aristocracy that was detaching itself more and more markedly from the mass of the people. In pursuing, as we shall have to do, the course of the struggle between the magnates and the king to its final outcome in the fifteenth century, we must not lose sight of other fields in which the endeavours and energies of Englishmen were finding expression.

As the political activities of the country gentlemen and even, to some extent, of the townsmen were being attracted into national channels by the competition between king and magnates for their support; as they learnt to use the opportunities presented by the concentration of representatives in a national assembly, so the habits of association and co-operation became more specifically concerned with non-political purposes. The community of the shire has, as it were, transferred its activities to the nascent House of Commons; but the communities of villagers, of burgesses, of craftsmen, of clerks, and of merchants are the more lively.

The township or village community has always been a natural unit for the common cultivation of the soil. Where a lord or squire possessed a considerable portion of the land, the villagers' activities had been to some extent subordinated to his purposes; but as his land was useless to him without their labour, he was bound to respect their traditions, as they were bound to acknowledge his claims if they wished to have the means of housing and feeding themselves. The custom of a manor represented the result of the give and take between these two interests.

Where there was no one lord, the community of the township emerged as an entity that could act for itself, regulating cultivation, passing by-laws, founding charities, building bridges, even going to law in the king's courts in the person of one or two villagers empowered to act on behalf of the whole community. But alongside its spontaneous activities the township might have to take action as a result of the responsibilities imposed on it by royal authority.

Thus when the squire of a Northamptonshire village killed the parson in the churchyard in the days of Edward I, the villagers did their duty by arresting him, and though he escaped from their custody, the royal justices recognized their position as keepers of the king's peace by sentencing the recaptured criminal to death on the charge not of murder but of jail breaking, for freeing himself from the detention of men who in all probability were his own serfs. The township that had to provide jurors for a coroner's inquest, to have ready weapons for home defence or for the keeping of the peace, and to provide night-watchmen; that could, moreover, be fined for the non-performance of these duties, was well aware of itself as a community.

As the thirteenth century advanced, there were many instances of the men of the village as a body buying privileges from the king, or renting the land of the manor from him or from some other lord to work it themselves. The village community, generally identical with the ecclesiastical parish, cared for its aged and invalid members, and when the Black Death had loosened the ties that bound men to their birthplaces, and the tramp seeking his fortune came on the scenes, responsibility for the able-bodied beggar also was fixed on the township by the statute of Cambridge, the oldest enactment in the code that grew into the Elizabethan Poor Law.

The law of the land was, in fact, readier to recognize the duties of the village than its rights; and the township failed to establish itself as an integral part of the political community. 'Day labourers and poor husbandmen, copy-holders and artificers,' says a writer in 1565, 'these have no voice or authority in our commonwealth, and no account is made of them but only to be ruled, not to rule other.' Local authority in the country-side came to be exercised not by elective officials chosen by the community, but by keepers and justices of the peace appointed by the central government—a body of country gentlemen who saw that the laws for regulating labour were enforced, and who were more careful to preserve public order than to safeguard the ancient rights of the villager to his share in the common pasture. When the manorial system ceased to meet the needs of agriculture, no agricultural corporation took its place; individual villagers who had made good secured and defended their individual rights as best they could.

The community of the borough had another fate. Whilst some of the little towns of the early Middle Ages failed to justify their existence as urban centres, a large number maintained and added to their privileges as chartered boroughs, and developed the appropriate organs for municipal government. To the bailiffs who linked them with the central government, and the mayor that their civic consciousness had created in imitation of the French communal practice, were added the town council, ultimately composed of aldermen, and the common council, a select body exercising most of the functions of the full assembly of burgesses, those townsmen who were members of the borough community.

At no time, it seems probable, had every resident in the borough been admitted to the body that enjoyed customary and chartered privileges, and in most boroughs the constitution grew steadily more oligarchic as time went on. Each borough had its own customs and governmental institutions. In some the earliest form of association had been the gild merchant or society of those allowed to trade in the town; in others the freemen of the borough court formed the oldest society. But commercial and legal privileges usually merged; and the community of the borough, however it originated, regulated the market, controlled trade, did justice, passed by-laws in regard to nuisances, and safeguarded the interests of its members when they came into conflict with those of other boroughs.

In the course of the fourteenth and fifteenth centuries, as

the status of corporations came to be established and defined by law, boroughs, like monasteries and colleges, became capable of owning property and of suing and of being sued in the law courts.

Within these urban communities other societies flourished. There were the religious gilds whose members worshipped together; friendly societies, serving the purpose of dining and burial clubs, concerned, that is, with the most familiar and intimate sides of the daily life of the town, and not unknown in the villages also. 'If any member die,' say the regulations of an early Cambridge gild, 'let the whole gildship bring him to the place he chose for burial, and he who does not come shall pay fifteen pints of honey; and the gildship will pay half the expense of the funeral feast and each shall give twopence in alms.' Two fourteenth-century Cambridge gilds of this kind combined to found Corpus Christi College.

More important, as being fellowships that did work and accepted responsibility on behalf of the whole town, were the craft gilds. These were made up of townsmen practising the same handicraft, and at once regulated admission to the trade and kept up the standards of workmanship. As manufacture grew more elaborate and division of labour increased, the number of craft gilds multiplied; there would be one for each of the four or five stages in the making of cloth or in the making of leather goods and so on. Each craft regulated the training of the young craftsman by fixing the duties and rights of the apprentices and their terms of service, and appointed its own inspectors. At first entirely self-governing, as time went on the craft gilds became subordinate to the municipal government, their ordinances being registered in the town records under the mayor's keeping. Some gilds occupied a key position in an industry and came to dominate the others; thus in London the great livery companies of the mercers, the leather sellers, the goldsmiths, the cloth workers, and the rest came to control the government of the city, so that the Lord Mayor was always chosen from one of them. Whereas at first an apprentice might look forward confidently to becoming a master craftsman and running his own workshop, as industry prospered the master employed so many workmen and the fees for the mastership became so heavy that many expert craftsmen were obliged to remain permanently in the position of journeymen or hired workmen, and these in their turn formed societies to protect their interests, comparable to modern trade unions.

Capitalism was in fact beginning to appear. The gilds had done their work—not only the work left or delegated to them by the borough government of guarding the growth of industry and maintaining its standards, but also a work like that of the older rural communities, of exercising the townsman excluded from the highest offices in the art of self-government. The House of Commons has been called the community of communities, and the men who took responsibility in their craft assemblies, no less than the mayor and his brethren on the bench, were educating the burgess communities for their work of co-operation with the knights of the shires in the Common House.

Of all the craft gilds of the Middle Ages the most enduring have been those that practised the craft of book learning. In our two ancient universities we can still see traces of the regulations for the term of years during which the apprentice was trained in the mystery of learning, the paternalistic provision for his moral and physical well-being, the searching test by which he qualified for the position of master of the arts he had studied, and for admission to the society of those accorded the right to practise the craft of teaching.

From the thirteenth century the communities of clerks at Oxford and Cambridge have maintained a continuous existence. The good learning, traditionally associated with godliness, which had thrown up the unorthodox Roger Bacon in the days of Henry III and the yet more unorthodox John Wyclif in the days of Edward III, which produced pioneer Protestants like Garret and Clark of Oxford and Gerard and Barnes of Cambridge, pioneer Renaissance scholars like Fisher and Linacre, founders of the Anglican tradition like Cranmer and Parker, and heroes of the Catholic reaction like Campion and Parsons, was almost miraculously preserved in the storm which wrecked the older communities of monks and friars, and

destroyed the parish gilds by stripping them of their modest
endowments.)

The later Middle Ages saw the development of communities
of merchants that were not localized as the twelfth-century
gilds merchant had been. English overseas trade had existed
from the days of Offa, and the Norman Conquest had established close relations with the cloth making county of Flanders,
as the Angevin conquest was to link England with the wine
growing regions of Gascony. But the trading companies active
in England in the thirteenth century are those of foreigners,
and the Englishmen who were exporting wool to the Continent
in the last years of Henry III—some four hundred and fifty
in number—seem to have worked independently of each other.

It was once again compulsion from above that instigated
common action and the acceptance of common responsibility.
The canalization of the export trade in wool seemed desirable
to the three Edwards on various grounds; to facilitate the
collection of customs, to make more easily accessible an ample
source of ready money, and to put at the king's disposal an
invaluable diplomatic bargaining counter. Edward I and
Edward II had from time to time appointed certain ' staple '
towns to which all wool for export must be brought; now in
England, now in various centres on the Continent.

Edward III took the further step of giving to the Company
of the Staple the monopoly of exporting wool, thus creating an
organization that would both manage the export trade and
serve as his bankers when he needed ready money. This threat
to the financial powers of the embryonic House of Commons was
defeated by the combined action of the smaller wool exporters
and the wool growers, who included men at every level of
English society from the peasant to the duke.

The monopolistic powers of the Staplers were destroyed
in 1353, but in the long run some such organization proved
the best for all parties, and at the end of the fourteenth century
the Company of the Staple was established with its headquarters
at Calais; a chartered company that in the course of the fifteenth
century came to farm the customs, to levy the wool subsidies
voted by parliament, and to advance loans to the government,

paying the wages of the garrison at Calais, managing a mint, and generally performing many of the functions of a government bank.

By the fifteenth century England had other valuable commodities to export besides wool. The well-to-do Flemish weavers whom Edward III had invited to England had given a fresh impetus to the cloth industry; establishments employing a large number of workmen were appearing in Suffolk and Essex, in Wiltshire, Devonshire and the Cotswolds, managed by the forerunners of the famous Jack of Newbury, who, according to the sixteenth-century ballad, had two hundred weavers working in one room.

Cloth was far and away the leading industrial export, but many other goods such as salt, iron, corn, beans, fish, hides, timber, and horses were transported overseas in the vessels of such great shipowners as William Canning, five times mayor of Bristol, who lies buried in St. Mary Redcliffe. He employed as many as eight hundred men in his ships, controlled about a quarter of all the shipping in the port of Bristol, and carried goods to Iceland, the Baltic, Spain, Portugal, France, and the Netherlands.

The traders who were associated for the export of these various commodities were the Merchant Adventurers. Though these gained their first privileges from foreign rulers, their standing as a group was recognized in England by charters from Edward III, Richard II, and Henry IV. They came into competition with alien merchants, especially with the Hanseatic league in the Baltic, and suffered a setback in the later fifteenth century, but under Henry VII they more than recovered lost ground. Henry established their status as an organized corporation by his charter of 1505, and also secured substantial advantages for them by his two treaties with Burgundy. Their members were found in all the greater ports—London, York, Newcastle, Hull, and Bristol—with local groups affiliated to the main corporation.

By the sixteenth century they had the monopoly of the general export trade, with membership open to all who had paid the admission fees and were willing to accept their authority. They were the precursors of the great Regulated

Companies that were later to open up trade with Turkey, Muscovy, and the Indies, and prepare the way for the overseas expansion of English empire.

As these various communities were in effect participating in the work of government, so no form of commercial or industrial activity was unaffected by royal policy. Nor did any notions of social prestige prevent the aristocracy from interesting themselves in commercial enterprise. The part played by the Staple in Edward III's foreign policy, the personal concern of the sons of Henry IV in trade with Ireland or with Gascony, as the case might be, the support given by the merchant staplers to Warwick the king-maker, who as captain of Calais made it the Yorkist headquarters in the years 1459–61, are all examples of the interweaving of economic and political threads in the web of history. The disorders of the fifteenth century, like the epidemics of the fourteenth, caused checks and setbacks; but none the less the work of the shepherds, the cultivators, the weavers, and the handicraftsmen was steadily accumulating those reserves of wealth that were to make possible the great efflorescence of Elizabethan England.

Round about 1350 an unknown poet contrasted the functions of the Winners and the Wasters; those who gained and guarded wealth, and those who spent it magnificently, whether in luxurious display or in warfare. The Waster taunts the Winner with his barren hoarding of goods:

When thou hast stored thy wide houses with wool-sacks full,
What should wax of that wealth, if no waste were to come?
Some would rot, some would rust, some rats would feed.
Let be the cramming of thy coffers, for Christ's love of heaven!
With our feasts and our farings we feed the poor.
Wouldst thou have lords to live as lads afoot?

The Winner retorts:

With thy stir and thy strife thou destroyest my goods,
In excess, in unthrift, in arrogance of pride.
Thou dightest to dine with dainties so many,
Twelve dishes at a time between two men;
But when this bliss is pass'd, the bill must be paid.

The exploits of the Wasters always make the more highly coloured story, but it is the Winners who advance the scope of human activity.

> Winner is the wight who all the world helpeth
> For folk from him learn, through leading of Wit.

Most of the communities of medieval England have done their work and passed away; they 'were but inns and resting-places,' but they left to those who should come after traditions of labour and effort in fellowship, of co-operation and the willing acceptance of responsibility for neighbours and colleagues, traditions that were to be caught up into the larger inheritance of the English commonwealth.

CHAPTER XI

ENGLISH MONASTICISM

No picture of English life in the Middle Ages is complete that leaves out monasticism. Of all the communities of medieval England the religious were those which were, for some eight centuries, most completely taken for granted as an integral part of society. Yet in origin the monks were fugitives from society. In the fourth century, the whole-hearted Christian found himself in a world in which the unconverted pagans outnumbered the Christians and the Christian community itself, no longer persecuted but protected by the Empire, had become the safe and respectable home of a crowd of time-servers. The prospect of a near end to things temporal had faded out; he was faced with a dilemma like that of the pacifist of to-day—how to put his faith into practice in a society that did not accept his standards and still remain an active citizen of that society. The first answer to the problem was the hermits', who fled to the Egyptian deserts and sought perfection in solitude. But it is not good for man to be alone, and very few can stand the strain of permanent isolation. A succession of experiments by men who had lived a good common life in their family or in a village or in the army issued ultimately in the Rule of St. Benedict, which laid down a pattern of religious life whose sanity and wisdom has made it for fourteen hundred years the standard of monastic communal life. The Benedictine Rule has been the parent of countless varying types of religious orders, but they are all based on the threefold vow of poverty, chastity and obedience to the abbot or father of the family. One reformer after another has returned to the fountain head to recover the balance between worship, work and study in the religious life.

The missionaries who came to Kent in 597 were monks from a Roman monastery, and Pope Gregory who sent them was himself a monk. Within ten years they had founded a monastery in Canterbury, St. Augustine's. Meanwhile the missionaries from Iona had brought another type of monasticism to Northumbria—a monasticism that had come from France to Scotland by way of Ireland and was 'more austere, less humane and more eremitical' than the Benedictine. Lindisfarne in the north, Glastonbury in the south, drew their inspiration from Celtic sources. In the pagan and barbarous England of the seventh century the monasteries were the bases for evangelism, and as Christianity spread, they became the nurseries of the church leaders and the centres of learning, art and culture. Bede tells how the Gregorian chants, the starting point of medieval music, were used and taught in the churches of Kent and Northumbria. Vernacular Christian poetry, as we have seen, was born at Whitby Abbey; the Lindisfarne gospels are here to-day to show what the monastic artist of the eighth century could achieve. Bede's writings bear witness to the well-stocked library of Jarrow. The education given in the monasteries was for children dedicated to the religious life by their parents; they learnt their letters and their psalter at the same time, following the monastic routine, though with a milder discipline. Alcuin writing from the court of Charlemagne to his former teachers at York thanks them for their patience and the fatherly care with which they chastised the heedless boy who preferred Vergil to the psalms, and 'made a man of him'.

By the year 800 there were at least one hundred monasteries in England, not to mention those in the Celtic regions of the island. Besides the houses in Northumbria and Kent there were Crowland, Ely and Peterborough in the fens, Pershore, Evesham and Gloucester in the Severn valley, Abingdon and Chertsey in the Thames valley, St. Albans on the Watling Street and Bermondsey and Barking near London. There were other small cells or *monasteriola*, like that in which St. Willibrord's father 'lived the religious life with his wife and all his household' near the mouth of the Humber. Eleven at least were double monasteries of men and women, presided over by an abbess like Hilda of Whitby: such were Barking, Wimborne, Repton and Much Wenlock. Some eight of the monasteries were also episcopal sees. No Christian of the eighth century would have conceived a church without monasteries. A movement that had begun as a flight from the world had become a source of learning and a centre of beneficence, and the monasteries of England, sending out their evangelists to the Continent, were the most vital and influential in Europe.

'For nearly three hundred and fifty years,' wrote Alcuin in 793 when he heard of the sack of Lindisfarne by the Danes, 'have we dwelt in this fairest of lands, and never before has such terror come on England as we are now enduring. St. Cuthbert's church, the most venerable in all Britain, sprinkled with the blood of priests and robbed of its ornaments, has become the spoil of the heathen.' This was but the first wave of the tempest that swept away not only the treasures of the monasteries but monasticism itself. Every monastery north and east of the Watling Street was utterly destroyed and, when Alfred became king, those of the south-west that survived no longer observed the Rule, but had become either the property of a layman or the lodgings of married clerics, like Glastonbury when Dunstan was a boy. Alfred, who had read Bede and knew what monasticism could be, founded Athelney as a house for monks and Wilton and Shaftesbury for nuns, but Athelney soon ceased to exist, and if the Rule was kept in the two nunneries it is probable that they and St. Augustine's in Canterbury were alone in preserving the regular life in England in the days when it was being revived on the Continent at Cluny and Fleury.

English monasticism was refounded by Dunstan who, like St. Augustine, was a scholar before he was a saint. Though there were no monks at Glastonbury it was a shrine to which pilgrims came, some of them learned men from Ireland, and the monastic library was still in existence. At first a student and later a member of Athelstan's household, Dunstan found himself called to the religious life, and when King Edmund made him titular abbot of Glastonbury in 943 he set to work to create a true monastery there, collecting disciples and instructing them in the Benedictine Rule. One of his monks, Aethelwold, was given the derelict abbey of Abingdon a year before Dunstan was banished by Edmund's son. In exile

Dunstan saw for himself the reformed monasticism in Ghent, and when Edgar recalled him in 957 and made him first Bishop of Worcester and London, and then Archbishop of Canterbury, he was able to bring about a rebirth of monasticism throughout England south of the Humber. The three monk-bishops, Dunstan, Oswald and Aethelwold, with King Edgar's whole-hearted support, refounded ancient abbeys like St. Albans, Peterborough and Malmesbury, and founded new houses like Ramsey and Sherborne.

It was a renaissance not only of the regular life but of the arts and letters associated with it in the past. Dunstan himself was a composer, an illuminator and a metalworker, who according to the traditions of Abingdon abbey made two great bells for them with his own hands. Aethelwold was also a skilled craftsman, and the monks of Ely were workers in gold and silver. The two Winchester monasteries gave their name to the school of illumination whose exquisite designs and beautiful lettering are as famous as the fresh and lively line drawings inspired by the famous Utrecht Psalter. The same freshness and liveliness appears in the writings of Aelfric, Abbot of Eynsham, not only in the vernacular homilies already mentioned, but in the Latin dialogues which he composed for the children of the monastery. He was clearly a born teacher: to help the boys to acquire a good Latin vocabulary he makes them take the part of different workers—the ploughman, the carpenter, the shoe-maker, the shepherd, the oxherd, the baker, the salter, the cook, the hunter, the fowler, the fisherman and the merchant, and finally pits them against each other in a debate as to which is the most important craft. The boy who impersonated the fisherman must have enjoyed answering the question, 'Do you wish to catch a whale?', as much as the mer-chant who is asked if he sells his goods at the same price for which he bought them overseas, or the cook who says, 'Without my craft you would not be able to bite your food.' And the boy who is asked 'Have you been beaten today?' and replies 'No, I was careful', and then to the question 'How about the other boys?' replies indignantly 'Why do you ask me? I can't tell you our secrets', is no remote figure. We learn also from him that the monastery children, though beating was in the Middle Ages an indispensable instrument of education, were treated tenderly in other respects. 'I still eat meat, because I am a child.' When he becomes a monk, the Rule will forbid meat-eating.)

The traditions of Jarrow and Wearmouth had been revived, but contact with the continental movement of reform led to something new: the framing of a standard rule for all monasteries covering monastic life in detail. The *Regularis Concordia*, drafted by Aethelwold and approved by an assembly of bishops, abbots and abbesses meeting at Winchester in 970, was endorsed by the king, who agreed to be the patron of all the men's houses as his wife would be of the women's. It was based on various continental models, but expressly preserved peculiarly English habits, such as prolonged bell ringing at Christmas and other feasts, open air church processions, and the election of the bishop of a monastic see by the monks.

In the century before the Conquest the monastic body had a share in the national life without parallel elsewhere. Most of the bishops were monks; and the abbots were present with them in the king's council. And owing to the generous gifts of land and of royal privileges by Edgar, Cnut and Edward the Confessor, many of the monasteries had acquired responsibilities of a secular order, for with the growth in power and responsibility of the monarchy Anglo-Saxon kings had more to give. So the great Benedictine abbeys of Peterborough, St. Albans, Ely, Bury St. Edmunds, Worcester, Glastonbury and Evesham acquired along with the right to royal tolls and royal profits of justice the duty of securing justice and peace for the dwellers on their lands. They, like the secular lords, were partners with the king in the concerns laid on him by his coronation oath.

In spite of the second wave of Danish invasion under Swein and Cnut, and the Confessor's choice of civil servants as well as monks to be bishops, English monasticism was still vigorous on the eve of the Conquest, notably in the west. Wulfstan of Worcester, the saintly friend of Harold, built up his monastery from twelve to fifty monks and Evesham, under Abbot Aethelwig, helped to send a mission to Northumbria

which refounded the ancient houses of Tynemouth, Wearmouth and Whitby, and later another that founded the
monastery of Odense in Denmark. Both abbots were honoured
and trusted by the Conqueror; Aethelwig, besides serving as
administrator of six shires, offered an asylum to the English
refugees driven from their homes by William's wasting of the
north.

The Norman Conquest meant no violent break in monastic
life. With only a few painful clashes the Norman abbots stepped
into the shoes of their English predecessors, and the two great
monk archbishops, Lanfranc and Anselm, brought with them
the strict standards and the religious fervour of Bec Abbey.
There was much building of abbey churches and some new
foundations, notably William's abbey of Battle on the site of
the battle of Hastings, and a few Cluniac houses founded by
Norman barons, such as Lewes and Castle Acre. But the great
impact from continental monasticism was to come later, and
in the long run the most important change brought by the
Conquest was damaging to the religious life. The uniform
imposition of feudal tenure meant that the abbeys like other
land-holders had to render secular services. Knights had to be
found for the king's army, the abbots had to attend the king's
council if summoned,[1] and worst of all, when an abbot died
the lands and revenues of the abbey were taken into the king's
hands until the new abbot was chosen and did homage. As the
kings often extended these profitable vacancies, even for years,
the monasteries countered by dividing the property of the house
between the convent and the abbot, so that only the abbot's share
was seized by the crown. An elaborate administrative system
developed in the larger and older houses, with officials for the
management of the two separate establishments, and the old
intimate relationship between the abbot and his monks, as
father of a family, was weakened if not destroyed.

In the twelfth century the monastic impulse reached a

[1]From the thirteenth century on this involved attendance at parliaments.
The number of abbots summoned varied considerably and some abbeys
bought exemption. When the monasteries were dissolved the removal of
the twenty-seven parliamentary abbots greatly changed the balance of the
House of Lords.

force never known before or since. It was the religious element
in that renaissance of life and thought which expressed itself
in urban life, in poetry, science and letters, and produced the
universities. Hitherto each religious house had been autono-
mous, save for the daughters of Cluny; now *orders*, each following its own special rule, came into existence. The first to win
wide support in England was the order of Black or Austin
Canons: communities of men in holy orders, bound to the
observance of a rule modelled on that of St. Augustine's
household. It was a judicious and humane rule: 'An elephant
can swim in it and a lamb can walk in safety.' Some of the
canons served churches, as no Benedictine monk could, and
many cared for the sick. St. Bartholomew's Hospital descends
from their house founded in 1123. Another of their four
London houses was endowed with rights over a whole City
ward, so that its prior was *ex-officio* alderman of Aldgate. Their
houses were small, but came to outnumber those of any other
order; forty were founded before the death of Henry I, the
king and his court being leading founders.

But by that date three other new orders were founding
houses in England. The Premonstratensian or White Canons
Regular, who followed a more austere rule than the Black; the
Gilbertines, whose English founder revived in a new form the
double monastery of the eighth century by setting up houses of
nuns with canons as chaplains and lay sisters and brothers to
serve them; and, foremost of all, the Cistercians, who set the
strongest stamp on twelfth-century England. They were the
spearhead of the monastic revival; their ideals and institutions
influenced not only the other new orders but the older Benedictine house.

Stephen Harding, an Englishman, was one of the founders
and the second abbot of Cîteaux, from which the order took its
name, and a number of Englishmen joined St. Bernard at
Clairvaux. The desire for a purer and stricter observance of
the Rule than they could find in any existing monastery drove
them and countless others to seek hardness and poverty in
remote and deserted places. The first Cistercian colony in
England was in Surrey; the invasion of the wilds of Yorkshire

began four years later. Rievaulx, whose English abbot came from Clairvaux, was founded in March 1132, and a few months later an exodus of monks from the too easy-going Benedictine house of St. Mary's at York settled at Fountains. Like Tintern and the Welsh houses of Valle Crucis and Strata Florida, both foundations were in lonely and desolate spots. Rievaulx, reinforced in 1133 by more emigrants from York, grew rapidly; under its saintly abbot Ailred (1147–67) it numbered 650 monks. In twelve years after their coming thirteen Cistercian houses had been founded. 'Men flocked to the Cistercians as in the nineteenth century they flocked to the goldfields.' Between 1135 and 1175 the number of English religious houses doubled; in 1100 there had been 88, in 1200 there were close on 400, most of them belonging to one or other of the new orders. Northern England was transformed by the coming of the Cistercians. In 1066 there had been no monasteries north of the Wash; in 1100 there were 6, most of them Evesham foundations; by 1200 there were 24 Cistercian houses, 15 of Gilbertines, 46 of Austin Canons and 16 of White Canons. In 1066 a sixth of the land of England was held by monasteries; in 1216 between a quarter and a third. The Cistercians had sought apostolic poverty and freedom from secular involvements. But their labours made the wilderness blossom like the rose, and the Yorkshire hills became covered with their sheep, so that Italian merchants came north for their excellent wool. St. Bernard himself, the most famous of early Cistercians, had been dragged back into the whirl of politics, and his English followers also found themselves involved in disputes resulting from the conflict of new standards with existing practices. The general chapter of the Cistercian order recognized the dangers of over-expansion by forbidding any further foundations in 1151.

One order escaped both popularity and its dangers—the Carthusian. The first house was founded in Somerset by Henry II as part of his penance for the death of Becket; its abbot Hugh, later Bishop of Lincoln, was his close friend. The Carthusian rule of silence and contemplation was even more austere than the Cistercian, and from Henry II to Edward III there were only two Charterhouses in England.

Between 1343 and 1414 seven were founded, seemingly as part of the movement towards the contemplative life which produced recluses and hermits like Julian of Norwich and Richard Rolle.[1] The London Charterhouse whose name survives to-day in the school was founded in 1371. It was said of the Carthusian order that 'it was never reformed because it was never deformed.' The last monks of the London house were among the few who paid the full price of martyrdom for their refusal to make any concession to Henry VIII.

The twelfth century had seen the 'most spectacular expansion of the monastic order which this country had ever witnessed.' But the impulse to the religious life was not yet exhausted; the thirteenth century saw the coming of the Friars —in 1221 the Dominicans, in 1224 the Franciscans, and later the Carmelites and Augustinians. St. Francis's ideal was literal obedience to those commands which Christ gave his earliest disciples. His followers were to have nothing of their own, not even books or community houses, and were to live on charity and their own labours. Primitive simplicity could not be preserved as his followers grew to thousands, and, in the event, it was obedience to the command to preach the gospel to all people that distinguished the followers of Francis, as of Dominic, whose first mission had been to convert the heretic. The legal device of the trust in this country probably owes its origin to the friars' wish to observe the letter of the law of poverty; the friars' houses which sprang up all over England[2] were held for the friars, not by them. The scholars and lawyers converted by the friars insisted that to preach they must study, and at both Oxford and Cambridge they forwarded the growth of the young universities by their distinguished scholarship.

It was by their evangelism that the friars added something new. St. Francis himself had had a struggle as to whether he should 'devote himself wholly to prayer or also to preaching', for in making service to the world of men their calling the friars were departing both from the original Benedictine ideal and from its

[1] See p. 173.
[2] By 1300 there were 55 Franciscan, 47 Dominican, 26 Carmelite and 17 Augustinian houses in England, most of them in towns.

Cistercian form. To quote Chesterton: 'What St. Benedict had stored, St. Francis scattered. The servants of God who had been a besieged garrison became a marching army.' Thirteenth-century England needed them and welcomed them. Their popularity as preachers and confessors led them to positions of influence. From Henry III to Henry VI all the English kings had friars for their confessors; they were valued diplomatists; and two became archbishops of Canterbury.[1] On the other hand, it also led to difficulties with the parish clergy who saw their flocks deserting them to listen to the friars. When Wesley and his followers preached the gospel to the poor in the eighteenth century they were driven out of the Church; in the thirteenth the bishops, notably Stephen Langton and Grosseteste of Lincoln, welcomed the friars as allies, and a succession of papal bulls upheld their right to preach against the jealousy of the parish clergy. The simplicity and saintliness of the first generation of friars here is unquestioned. In 1240 the Minister-General of the Franciscans on his deathbed praised the English above all other nations for their zeal for the Order.

Monasticism reached its climax in the twelfth century and the impulse to new forms of the religious life died down after the coming of the friars. The standards set in the early days of both movements were not maintained. Cistercians and Franciscans alike found the truth of the saying 'Woe unto you when all men shall speak well of you!' Great popularity and great numbers alike militated against poverty and simplicity. They were trusted, and so they were used; they were honoured, and great and small poured gifts on them. To live in the world, as the friars had to do, and remain unspotted by it proved impossible. Their latest and most just historian has to speak of the 'decent mediocrity' of both monks and friars in the century before the Black Death, and of their 'flavour of the commonplace' in the following century. The standards of observance went downhill; the visitors of the earlier period had removed unworthy heads of houses, in the fifteenth century they were merely reprimanded.

The numbers of the religious declined correspondingly. In

[1] Kilwardby, a Dominican, 1273; Pecham, a Franciscan, 1279.

1150, it is estimated, there were about 13,000 monks, canons and nuns; in 1300, in a population of some three millions, 17,500, including friars. The Black Death reduced them to 8,000 in a population of about two millions, but by the reign of Henry VII there were over 12,000. Under Henry V, a would-be reformer of monasticism, there had been the beginnings of a revival. He founded a Carthusian monastery at Richmond and opposite it, across the river, a house for nuns, priests and lay brothers of the new Swedish Bridgettine order—Syon, famous for its library and for the eloquence of its preachers, whom the fashionable world of London came out to hear in the early sixteenth century.[1] The new foundations, like Eton and King's College at a later date, were endowed with property taken from the alien priories closed down in 1414. Henry even drafted new articles for the Benedictine order. But he died before he could found his third house, and the reforming impulse died with him.

There were contemporary critics of the monks and friars from the reign of Henry II onwards. The bright young men of the literary renaissance abused them savagely. Giraldus Cambrensis charged the Benedictines with gluttony and loose living; Walter Map called the Cistercians masters of avarice, who laid waste the countryside to make a solitude for themselves. Personal grudges may account for their bitterness. And the bishops who about the same time attacked particular monasteries resented the papal privileges which had exempted them from episcopal control. In the thirteenth century Matthew Paris, himself a Benedictine, had nothing good to say of the friars. In the fourteenth Chaucer gives us portraits of the hunting monk, the plausible and greedy friar, and the pretty, fashionable little prioress. Langland, whilst paying tribute to St. Francis himself, depicts both friars and monks in very similar fashion. His is the indignation of a sad and serious poet, and it is he who makes the famous prophecy of the chastisement to come on the religious for breaking of their rule, so that nuns,

[1]Syon Abbey, now in Devon, is the only English religious community which has preserved its continuity unbroken, through exile and return, from the Middle Ages to the present day.

monks and canons 'shall have a knock of a king, and incurable the wound'. Fitz Ralph, Archbishop of Armagh, inveighed against the privileges of the friars; and Wyclif, most drastic of all the critics, in a mounting torrent of invective, demanded the complete abolition of all religious orders. No one before Wyclif had questioned the validity of the monastic ideal. The most scathing critics of the religious had accepted it as good; it was their failure to live up to it, above all to the rule of poverty, for which they were blamed.

There were other circumstances contributing to the decline of monasticism, however, for which the monks and friars could not be held responsible. The very multiplication of the monasteries and orders, it has been said, acted as a diluting rather than a strengthening agent, and the founders were generally laymen. Again, especially in the case of the smaller foundations, the resources of the house were not adequate to meet the expenses of maintaining the fabric. Some decayed and disappeared. More significant was the rise of other agencies to do the work which the monks had done. Before the Norman Conquest there were no schools outside the monasteries; after it only monks and future monks were educated there. Other boys had their schooling from the parish priest, or from one of the new schools beginning to be founded. And for older students new centres of learning were coming into being, shifting with the movements of the famous scholars who taught there. We hear of the schools of Exeter, of Lincoln, of Northampton, and more and more often of Oxford, till it becomes a university towards the end of the twelfth century, soon to be followed by Cambridge. In the twelfth century others besides Alexander Nequam, the mathematician and astronomer, entered a monastery to pursue their studies in peace, and a scholar writes to a young friend, 'I do not advise you to seek a school or a master elsewhere than in a cloister. What place is better suited to study?' St. Albans, later to be famous for its historians, was such a house of learning under the three Angevin Kings. One abbot built up a library; another had studied medicine at Salerno; another had been at Paris, and besides cherishing both letters and medicine, attracted to the abbey artists and craftsmen who became monks. But in the thirteenth century the tide was flowing the other way. The friars were flocking to the universities, and the abbeys were sending their monks there. At Worcester College, Oxford, the row of small separate lodgings still in use formerly housed the monks from the different Benedictine abbeys that supported the college. The Exchequer and Chancery and the law courts were also training expert clerks. The monasteries were no longer needed for the work of education, and the great scholars were found elsewhere. Again, the leaders of the Church were no longer monks. Down to the end of Henry II's reign all the archbishops of Canterbury had been Regulars, except Becket, the civil servant; after that date only one monk and two friars became archbishops.

But although the monasteries no longer dominated spiritual and intellectual life, they still had much to give to the world outside their walls, and modern England is deeply indebted to them. We owe it to monastic scribes that we can read Horace, Cæsar and Tacitus; comparatively few classical manuscripts are older than the eighth century. From the age of Alfred to that of Richard II almost all the chronicles were written in monasteries. To Peterborough and Dunstable, to Winchester, Burton, Bridlington and many more, above all to St. Albans, the home of Roger of Wendover, of Matthew Paris and of Walsingham, the debt of the historian is incalculable. From the monasteries, too, came biographies, collections of letters, and transcripts of charters and other official documents of the days before systematic record keeping began in the government departments. The economic historian of medieval England goes to the monk's surveys and account rolls for information as to agriculture, estate management, wages and prices.

Very little literary material was left by the nunneries. They were mostly smaller and poorer, and they were far fewer.[1] Nuns were not as a rule learned, and their services to the poor and sick went unrecorded. But the very fact that women 'understand Latin with difficulty' meant that religious works were written for them in English, and these kept alive the tradition

[1] At the time of the dissolution of the monasteries there were about 140 nunneries and 815 houses for men in England.

of English prose writing. King Edgar and his wife requested Aethelwold to translate the Rule of St. Benedict for the use of reformed nunneries like Shaftesbury and Barking, and it was retranslated into Middle English in the fourteenth century. In the twelfth century, when French had almost superseded English for the politer classes, the *Rule of Anchoresses* was written in English for three women, possibly the daughters of a London citizen, who planned to lead the religious life together. For at least three hundred years the book 'enjoyed a prodigious popularity'. It was followed by a succession of devotional works and lives of the saints written for women in the mother tongue. Their language helped to form the tradition of religious prose that lies behind Tyndale's, and so behind 'King James's' Bible.

Very great, again, was the contribution of monasticism to medieval architecture. Sixteen of our present-day cathedrals were monastic churches down to the dissolution.[1] The splendours of Durham and Canterbury are part of our national heritage, but the monastic builders were craftsmen as well as artists. It was the Durham architects who solved 'the great problem of medieval architecture—how to construct and keep up a ribbed vault, oblong in plan, over a central aisle'. The long nave which we see at Canterbury, Winchester, Ely, St. Albans and Norwich and elsewhere, without parallel abroad, resulted directly from the monks' ceremonial of processions on Sundays and feastdays; and this influenced the architecture of non-monastic cathedrals such as Salisbury and Old St. Paul's. It was in Gloucester Abbey Church, as many hold, that what we call perpendicular architecture was born in the mid-fourteenth century, and the fan vaulting in the Gloucester cloister, where the monks' stone writing-desks are still to be seen, is the earliest example of the style which Henry VI's architects were to use at King's College and Eton, and Henry VII's at Windsor. The lantern of Ely, 'one of the most original and poetic conceptions of the Middle Ages', was Prior Alan of

[1]Canterbury, Chester, Coventry, Durham, Ely, Gloucester, Norwich, Peterborough, Rochester, St. Albans, Winchester and Worcester were the churches of Benedictine houses; Bristol, Carlisle, Oxford and Southwark of Austin Canons.

Walsingham's solution of a practical problem—'like all the best things in Gothic architecture'. Again, in the ruins of Fountains, Kirkstall and Tintern we can see how the puritanical reaction of the Cistercians against the over-ornate Romanesque architecture of the twelfth century, so fiercely expressed by St. Bernard, resulted in the severe and lovely simplicity of Early English mouldings. Their remoteness saved these ruins from the destruction and plunder which levelled to the ground the magnificent churches of Lewes, Hailes, Glastonbury, Shaftesbury and many more. Outside the cathedrals, only a few monastic churches have been preserved for worship, such as Tewkesbury, Romsey, St. Bartholomew's, Smithfield, and the royal Abbey of Westminster.

In the work of Church government the share of the monks was never again as great as it had been in the days of Dunstan. In the century before the Conquest more than half the bishops were monks. From William the Conqueror to John something like one in six, and from 1216 to 1485 something like one in seven, were monks. But a lasting legacy from Anglo-Saxon times was the cathedral monastery. The cathedrals of Worcester and Winchester were the churches of monastic bodies from the days of Oswald and Aethelwold, and when Lanfranc, seeing the monks as his chief helpers in the work of ecclesiastical reform, made Christchurch the cathedral monastery of Canterbury, other bishops followed his lead and by the end of the twelfth century more than half the cathedral chapters were monastic,[1] a system almost peculiar to England, which endured to the Reformation. But as time went on a cleavage between convent and bishop developed; the bishop concerned himself very little with the monks of the cathedral, who looked to their prior as their head, and though they still claimed to elect the bishop,[2] even this ceased to be effective as the system of papal provision practically superseded election in the fourteenth century.

A more lasting legacy from monasticism, and one of

[1]Canterbury, Bath, Carlisle, Coventry, Durham, Ely, Norwich, Rochester, Winchester and Worcester.

[2]The disputed election by the monks of Christchurch, in 1205, led to John's quarrel with the pope. See p. 96.

dubious value, was the system of vicarages. The earliest rural churches were regarded as the property of those who had built and endowed them, and many devout benefactors, especially, in the century after the Norman Conquest, bestowed their churches on monasteries as did collegiate foundations and cathedral chapters. By 1166 one in four of the parish churches of England were owned by religious houses, and it became a general practice for them, like the other corporate bodies, to appropriate to themselves the tithe payable for the support of church and priest, and to put in a salaried *vicar* to do the work of the parish—not a monk, but a secular priest. Thus, when at the dissolution the property of the monasteries came into lay hands, a lay 'rector' stepped into the shoes of the monks and became the recipient of the 'great tithes'.

Hospitality to the traveller and relief to the poor and sick were taken for granted as monastic obligations from the time of St. Benedict, and the guest house was a regular feature of the abbey buildings. As in California under the Spanish, the monasteries were indispensable hostelries. A house like St. Albans on the Watling Street was a regular port of call for royal and noble visitors as well as for less distinguished travellers and pilgrims. The expenses of such entertainment could be heavy; Lanercost was impoverished for years by the visit of Edward I in 1306-7, and in the fifteenth century the St. Albans chronicler writes of a royal duke who spent his Christmas there with 300 attendants. Even the comparatively remote Cistercian abbey of Beaulieu near Southampton Water spent nearly £120 in one year in entertaining guests.

As for the relief of the sick and poor there can be little doubt that down to the twelfth century, if no later, the main burden was borne by the monasteries. The almoner was a regular official with a fixed income for distribution in the neighbourhood. At Abingdon in the twelfth century he had a tenth of all the bread baked in the abbey to distribute. The surplus food from the tables of the abbot and monks was regularly given away. At many houses pensioners were supported; over 60 at Evesham, 43 at Bury St. Edmunds. At Beaulieu thirteen had lodging every night, and at Christmas and other feasts the poor guests equalled the number of the monks. During the miseries of Stephen's reign several wealthy houses sold their treasures to feed the starving. As to hospitals, they were founded, but not as a rule maintained, by the monks.

But in this as in other respects the picture changes in later centuries. Hospitals unconnected with monasteries were being founded from the twelfth century onwards. And it must be remembered that by canon law the first responsibility for poor relief lay on the parish, sometimes depleted of funds by monastic appropriation. The part played by the monasteries in relieving the poor on the eve of the dissolution has been exaggerated. The latest writer on medieval poor law is of the opinion that the English poor were better looked after in the thirteenth century than in any other before the twentieth.

The story of monasticism in medieval England is one of high achievement and human failure. The monastic ideal holds in itself the permanent tension of the Christian life. The refusal to live by sub-Christian standards drives the monk into isolated communities; the desire to translate love for his neighbour into action drives him back into the world, for they are few indeed who can fulfil their service by intercession alone. To the innumerable services that, as we have seen, the religious rendered to medieval England we must add this: that they were a living witness to a standard below which they inevitably fell when the tide of communal fervour ebbed. The men who prayed were to the Englishman of the Middle Ages as indispensable a part of the community as those who fought and those who laboured.

CHAPTER XII

MONARCHY VERSUS ARISTOCRACY
1297–1399

THE crisis of 1297 had seen the first unequivocal formulation of the constitutional doctrine that all forms of direct and indirect taxation should receive the consent of the taxpayers. As an event in political history, it marked the first mutterings of the storm that was in the fourteenth century to beat upon the English monarchy, to sweep two kings from their thrones, and so to weaken the royal power that it had to be reborn in a new and outwardly autocratic guise under the Yorkists and Tudors.

In the last ten years of Edward I's reign there were signs of the growing reaction against his system of bureaucratic government. Protests were being made in his parliaments against the power of the royal household, its requisitioning of supplies, its encroachments on the common law courts, and its supersession of the Exchequer in finance. The elected representatives of the communities were being drawn into the dispute and induced to present the grievances of the great men in the form of petitions to the king and his council; and the king was driven to defend his prerogatives by alleging that his coronation oath bound him to uphold the rights of the crown and by obtaining, like his father and his grandfather, papal absolution from the promises extorted by his subjects.

Some of the baronial leaders were immobilized by skilful diplomacy and ingenious marriage settlements, but when Edward died his son was confronted by forces quite beyond his power to control.

Edward II was a cheerful and irresponsible amateur at the craft of kingship; he was faced by a coalition of his father's displaced servants, of the serious and responsible heads of the great departments, and of barons determined to end his father's system, led by his cousin, Thomas Earl of Lancaster, and by the archbishop who had inspired the clerical opposition in 1297, and suffered for it at the hands of king and pope.

Thomas of Lancaster, heir to the lands and traditions of Simon de Montfort, had none of his high principle or persistence. The Ordinances of 1311, drawn up by himself and the archbishop with nineteen fellow magnates, restricted the king's activities, indicated parliaments as the proper occasions for political decisions and for the highest judicial activity, and subordinated the Household to the older departments, making its officials equally responsible to public censure; but the labours that membership of the council meant for the baronial leaders were too strenuous for Lancaster.

While the great officials continued the good work by a series of excellent regulations for Household and Exchequer, and thus secured the country against the dangers of a bureaucratic monarchy such as the French kings were establishing in France, the earl and his headstrong allies chose the fatal short cut of armed force. In 1312 they captured and executed without trial the royal favourite who was their chief bugbear. Ten years later the fortune of war favoured Edward II; Thomas of Lancaster, defeated, taken prisoner, and condemned as a traitor, was beheaded outside his own castle of Pontefract, and the Ordinances of 1311 were revoked by parliamentary statute.

In another five years Thomas's brother was backing with all his influence the venture of Edward's queen and her lover, Mortimer, in overthrowing Edward II and replacing him by his fourteen-year-old son, the third Edward; and the commons were petitioning the king to promote the canonization of Thomas, the hero of the Ordinances, before whose picture miracles had been wrought on the poor folk of London. Though the pope failed to respond to the reiterated requests of the young king and of Thomas's brother, the popular canonization of opposition to the crown had come to stay. So, more fatally, had the vendetta. The deposed king was murdered by Mortimer's orders in 1327; his half-brother, tricked into a plot to restore him, was executed in 1330; and Mortimer's own well-deserved execution as a traitor followed six months later.

Mortimer, unlike Lancaster, was condemned by his peers in parliament; and it was at a parliament that the common folk accepted Edward III as king in place of his father. In the twenty years of Edward II's reign, it had been established that matters which concerned the estate of the king and the realm should be treated in parliaments. It had also become the invariable rule that representatives should be summoned to every parliament.

The community of the realm was no longer a purely feudal or baronial entity; though knights and burgesses might at times disclaim responsibility and attempt to leave high matters of policy to the great men, the barons and the bishops were well aware of the advantages of involving as many as possible in such transactions as royal depositions or political trials.

Edward III, initiated into government by the men who had deposed his father, came into conflict with his baronage on one occasion only. For the greater part of his long reign of fifty years he and they made common cause in pursuing the French venture, but there was one episode at the outset of the war when he revived the technique of his grandfather, and attempted to use the Household organization not merely as a War Office but as a substitute for Chancery and Exchequer.

In 1338 he went off to France, after issuing a series of ordinances which subordinated the state departments in England to the group of Household officials who accompanied him abroad. In the crisis he had thus provoked lords, commons, and officials all took action. The Exchequer officials staged something like a go-slow strike; they 'regretted their inability' to collect the revenues needed for the king's wars.

When Edward suddenly returned, dismissed a number of leading officials, and summoned the ex-chancellor, that Archbishop Stratford who had taken a leading part in his father's deposition, to answer in the Exchequer for alleged peculation, Stratford claimed his privilege as a peer and was backed by the lay magnates. Their *esprit de corps* expressed itself further by a successful protest against the attendance in parliament of certain influential Household officials.

Edward had offered inducements to the shires to back him against the Exchequer, the Local Government Board of medieval England, but they showed no enthusiasm for the concessions he offered, and when requested to grant a tax for the king's urgent military needs, the representatives, regardless of the full power they were supposed to have, said they must consult their constituents. Faced by this combined resistance, maintained from 1339 to 1341 in a succession of parliaments, Edward yielded; gave his consent to statutes safeguarding the right of the lords to be judged by their peers in parliament, and in return for a grant of money agreed that his ministers should be sworn in parliament and answer to parliament for their official actions, and that account should be given in parliament of moneys granted in parliament.

When the last parliament was over he revoked the statutes, declaring that they infringed his coronation oath. But in fact he had learnt his lesson; successful war was impossible without the willing co-operation of both lords and commons, and from this time on the royal council included a growing number of the lords, whilst the rule that statutes could only be revoked by those who had passed them was upheld by Edward's action being sanctioned in the next parliament.

The war with France, arising in the first place from the chronic problem of the feudal relationship of the two kings, and from the aid given by Philip of France to the Scots, became a national issue when, in 1337, Edward III took the title 'King of France,' which, with true English conservatism, his successors were to retain to 1801. Diplomacy and economic pressure were called into play; alliances with the insurgent townsmen of Flanders against their count, with the rulers of the various Netherlandish states, with the emperor, with the claimant to the county of Brittany, in short, with any enemy of the French kings, were followed up by the surprise invasion of 1346 and the victories of Crecy and Calais.

The catastrophic disaster of the Black Death averted a reply in kind from France, and weakened both parties. It was the incompetence of the French king rather than military genius which gave the Black Prince his victory at Poitiers, the event which marks the lowest ebb of French fortune, when their king was taken prisoner. But the extravagance of the conquerors' demands defeated its own ends; the war had become a matter of prestige and a permanent peace proved unattainable.

The tide turned when Charles V became king of France in 1364, and a series of English reverses showed up the weakness of their strategy. The French provinces revolted against their governor, the Black Prince, and by 1380, of all the conquests of his father and grandfather, Richard II only retained Calais, Cherbourg, Bordeaux, and Bayonne. Yet even then the obviously sensible policy of peace was unpopular in both countries, and only in the teeth of baronial opposition and after long endeavours was Richard able to negotiate the truce that endured from 1396 to 1415.

Barren and demoralizing as the struggle was in the long run, it had served as a bond of union between the king and his subjects. The fighting classes, whether lords or squires, gambled gleefully on the chance of making a fortune from prisoners' ransoms; financiers and contractors became rich by providing loans and supplies; the knights and burgesses in parliament seized the opportunity to establish their right to grant the taxes on wool and other commodities and to put an end to private agreements between the king and the great merchants.

It was, in fact, the French wars that secured to the commons the exercise of those financial functions which were, in the long run, to make parliament the sovereign power in our constitution. The magnates shared Edward's pride in his French victories with the citizens and country folk who listened to despatches from France in the days of youthful exuberance celebrated by Froissart, with his blending of cruelties and courtesies. But as the century advances, and the Black Death is succeeded by constantly recurring bouts of the plague, the note changes. In place of the light-hearted jingoism of the *Vows of the Heron*, we hear the minor key of Langland's stern and mystical *Vision of Piers Plowman*, haunted by the consciousness of social wrong and economic grievance that was to find tumultuous expression in the rising of 1381.

The gallant young victor of Sluys and Crecy was sinking into senile depravity, and abandoning the reins of government to his third son, John of Gaunt. His eldest son, the Black Prince, who had won his spurs as a boy under his father's eyes in 1346, had returned in 1372 from the hopeless task of regaining Guienne, mortally ill, to spend his last days in attempting to overthrow the power of his younger brother.

The so-called Good Parliament of 1376 is a landmark in parliamentary history, not only because it saw the first use of the technique of impeachment—the collective accusation by the commons of men charged with notorious offences against the community, to be judged by the lords in the high court of parliament—but also because we have, for the first time, an eyewitness's account of the discussions of the knights and burgesses in their own traditional meeting place, the Chapter House of Westminster Abbey.

The official parliamentary rolls record the king's speech to the lords and commons, the archbishop's sermon, the petitions presented by individuals, by communities, or by the whole body of the commons to the king and the lords in parliament, but they have nothing to say about the proceedings of the lesser men when they left the parliament chamber and discussed among themselves what grant they would make to the king. But the unknown chronicler of 1376 depicts for us a well-established procedure: we see one member after another going to the abbot's lectern, first murmuring a blessing, and then making his speech; we note the reactions of the listeners to their eloquence; we recognize the man with a head on his shoulders who sums up and formulates public opinion, and who turns out, by a coincidence, to be the steward of the Earl of March, the Black Prince's nephew and agent in the lords' house. A conference with a select group of lords is described, and the bold demeanour of the commons' spokesman when he brings before the king and the magnates in parliament the grievances and denunciation of the listening commons. It is clear that a new political weapon is being forged.

In the thirty years that followed the death of Edward III, the rival factions were waging their wars in successive parliaments as well as outside, and diplomatic or military triumphs were being endorsed and legalized by the judgment of the lords in the king's highest court. How far the commons were consciously or unconsciously exploited by the lords, how far they took a line of their own, it is not easy to say. Country gentlemen of substance and ability undoubtedly influenced their lords and patrons, and where the interests of lords and commons conflicted, as over matters of local government or labour problems, there are signs of independence.

But the peerage had by 1376 become a well-defined and steadily narrowing ring of hereditary magnates, and the elected members of a parliament had only a few weeks in which to acquire the common consciousness that would enable them to act for themselves in a political issue. So the factions led by great earls, royal dukes, and even, at times, by the king himself, formed currents guiding the stream of public opinion in different directions. The leaders were accused of influencing elections; the parliament of 1377, which undid the work of that of 1376, was said to be packed by John of Gaunt, and both Richard II and his opponents certainly tried to bring pressure on the shire courts at elections. On the other hand, it was probably quite possible to get adequate backing from any collection of representatives, so great was the power of patronage, wealth, and influence in the England of the fourteenth and fifteenth centuries.

The Black Prince's son, Richard II, did his best to stand up against this phalanx of aristocratic influence, his most trying subject being the youngest of his three surviving uncles, Thomas of Gloucester. The magnates who ran the government in his minority authorized the ill-devised poll taxes of 1379 and 1380 which helped to precipitate the rising of 1381. But the country gentlemen must share the responsibility, for they had approved the detested Statute of Labourers, aimed at stabilizing wages and prices, and immobilizing labour in the confused economic conditions that followed the Black Death of 1349. The fifteen-year-old Richard showed instinctive ability in handling the rebels, many of whom had raised the standard of revolt in his name, but he had no power to mitigate the savage penalties inflicted in parliament and by the justices in the shires.

When later he tried to assert himself, he found how many of the weapons formerly wielded by the crown were now in the hands of the magnates. When he tried to invalidate the proceedings of parliament by absenting himself, a deputation reminded him that his great-grandfather had been deposed and that there were plenty of princes of the blood royal available to fill his place. When he appealed to arms, he found the opposition had better generals.

When he called upon the judges to define his royal rights, and to declare that the setting-up of a commission to overhaul the administration was treasonable, he found himself out-manœuvred; his judges in their turn were impeached as traitors, along with the faithful servants he had sought to protect. When, once again, the legal experts declared the methods used in parliament irregular, the lords retorted with the round statement that parliament was the highest court in the land and that no court, or judge, or jurist could pronounce upon its actions. The Merciless Parliament of 1388, the longest yet held, ended with a vote of thanks and a generous honorarium to the noble lords who had adjudged to death the most loyal of the king's supporters, in his name, and at the accusation of his faithful commons.

It looked as if Richard, like his grandfather in 1342, had learned his lesson. For some ten years he worked in co-opera-tion with his uncles, his cousins, and their adherents, in council and in parliament, handling ecclesiastical, economic, and military business with no very obvious differences arising. Then, in 1397, he hit back suddenly, arresting his uncle, Thomas of Gloucester, and the popular general, Arundel, who had been the leaders in the Merciless Parliament. The one was privately murdered in prison, the other tried in parliament and executed.

Other ringleaders were banished or imprisoned for life, and the docile or intimidated commons agreed to statutes revoking the acts of the Merciless Parliament and creating new and sweeping categories of treason. The king had copied the technique of his opponents, it would seem successfully. But in his desire to make assurance doubly sure, he overreached himself. He bound lords and commons with an unprecedented oath not to undo the work of 1397.

Half the counties of England were so terrified at the sweeping terms and retrospective force of his treason act that they bought provisional pardons from him. Moreover, he had an explicit theory of despotism, as no other English ruler had till the days of James I. The law was in his mouth and in his breast, he was reputed to have said, and the lives and lands of his subjects were his to do what he pleased with. The plain man, who concerned himself little with the disputes of dukes, and cared not a rap whether Thomas of Gloucester was alive or dead, was keenly sensitive to the suggestion that his property was no longer safeguarded by the old and familiar common law. And when Richard proceeded to put his principles into practice on the death of John of Gaunt by disinheriting his son Henry, a political opponent whom he had ostensibly pardoned, the fears and sympathies of all England were aroused.

What had happened to Henry of Derby, who ought to be Henry of Lancaster, might happen to anyone. His cause was the cause of all; and when he landed in Yorkshire in 1399 to claim his inheritance he found himself a popular hero, and the way was open for him to claim not only his duchy but the throne of England.

As in 1327 and in 1688, it proved difficult to legalize a revolution. The representatives summoned to Westminster by Richard's parliamentary writs were induced to act as an assembly of estates, to approve the deposition of a king who was declared to have violated his coronation oath by failing to do justice and uphold the law, to authorize the solemn surrender of their fealty to Richard by a delegation modelled on that sent to Edward II seventy-two years earlier, and to accept as their king Henry of Lancaster, who claimed the vacant throne as the lawful heir.[1]

---

[1] Henry's claim through his mother, based on a cock-and-bull story that Edward I was a younger son, was probably meant to exclude the Earl of March, Richard's presumptive heir and the ancestor of the Yorkist line.

Next week the same representatives met as the commons in Henry IV's first parliament and endorsed the revolution by statute. Richard had been tricked by Henry into surrender, and had been kept in the Tower while his fate was determined in Westminster Hall, under the glorious roof then fresh from the hands of his workmen. Now he was transferred to the north country castle where Thomas of Lancaster had been beheaded in 1322, there to perish himself within the year.

CHAPTER XIII

THE DECLINE AND FALL OF FEUDALISM

I

FROM ARISTOCRACY TO ANARCHY
1399–1461

THE overthrow of Richard II used to be acclaimed as a triumph of constitutionalism. It is true that the acceptance of his theory that the crown could override common law would have destroyed the safeguards of English liberties, but it is not possible to maintain that the triumph of Henry of Lancaster established the supremacy of parliament in the government of England. Henry claimed from the first to have all the royal rights Richard had had, and after 1399, as before, parliaments could be used to sanction whatever measures an aristocratic faction or an autocratic king could effectually recommend. It was not democracy but oligarchy that defeated Richard.

In the long struggle between king and baronage extending from 1215 to 1399, the baronage had won for the time being. As male heirs failed, and heiresses carried their lands to another line, the number of leading nobles had diminished and their wealth increased, setting them more at a distance socially from the knightly class. The accumulation of earldoms and estates held by John of Gaunt in the fourteenth century, or by Warwick the king-maker in the fifteenth century, are instances of the wealth which led Sir John Fortescue in 1471 to desiderate a kind of two-power standard for the English king: his wealth ought to be double that of his greatest subject, for wealth meant power.

Scarcely was Richard out of the way when Henry IV was faced by a rising of the Percies, those great north-country magnates whom he had induced to support him in 1399, and whose loyalty he had hoped to secure by lavish gifts of land. The defeat of the Percies at Shrewsbury in 1403 did not end Henry's difficulties; his own sons were to be almost as troublesome in his council as the uncles of Richard II had been in his. He found it no easier than Richard had done to get grants from his parliaments to replace the wealth with which he had bought support. The council, with more and more complex administrative duties, was hampered rather than controlled by the rules laid down in parliaments. The balance between aristocrats and civil servants on it varied with the power of the king; when the king was weak, the magnates gained ground.

A tired and disillusioned Henry IV was succeeded after fourteen years by his stern and vigorous son, who bettered his great-grandfather's achievements both at home and abroad. He was master in his own house; he led a reluctant aristocracy into war; but once it was fairly started the rivalry between king and magnates was suspended as they both plunged joyfully into a renewed French enterprise in which the victory of Agincourt, followed up by the diplomatic triumph of the Burgundian alliance and the conquest of Normandy, was crowned by the treaty of 1420 which gave the English king, together with the hand of the French king's daughter, the reversion of the throne of France.

The premature death of Henry V, followed almost at once by that of his father-in-law, left his nine-month-old son king of France and England, but cut short the process of establishing effective royal control of government. Once again the magnates, for the most part royal uncles or royal cousins, found themselves in a position to dominate council and parliament.

The unhappy child who was crowned at Westminster and Paris inherited from his French grandfather not only a divided kingdom and a disputed throne, but also a mental instability which made of his reign one long minority. The gentle and saintly founder of Eton and King's College who urged on the pope the canonization of Alfred the Great had no taste or gift for government. As a child, he was the helpless spectator of the feuds and rivalries of his uncles, the brothers of Henry V, and their Beaufort half-brothers, the legitimized descendants of John of Gaunt, whilst his uncle's death only cleared the stage, after 1447, for the quarrels between his French wife, Margaret of Anjou, with her Beaufort and de la Pole allies, and Henry's cousin, Richard, Duke of York, the acknowledged heir to the throne until the birth of a son to Henry in 1453.

Henry's French kingdom, ably administered by his uncle, John of Bedford, never covered much more than Normandy; and even in Normandy English rule was resented, and an underground movement existed well before Joan of Arc appeared in 1429 to rouse French national feeling and to secure the coronation of a French king at Rheims. She was captured and burned, and little Henry taken over to Paris to be crowned, but English rule in France was doomed. Henry V had taxed England's resources too heavily for her to be able to maintain the efforts that national pride demanded.

Inch by inch the French lands were lost; the unpopular marriage treaty of 1445 registered the loss of almost all that Henry V had won, and when the defeat and death of the English commander at Chatillon ended the fighting in 1453, the last remains of Eleanor of Aquitaine's inheritance had gone, and of the conquests of Edward III only Calais remained.

Two years after the fighting in France ended, it began in England. The battle of St. Albans, fought between the adherents of Richard of York, who had been appointed protector of the realm during Henry's temporary insanity, and those of the queen and Edmund Beaufort, heralded in thirty years of intermittent civil war. A French chronicler explains the situation simply by saying that the English lords were so used to fighting and looting, that when they could no longer make their fortunes in France, they fell upon each other's lands in England. English historians have noted that every truce with France let loose on England a number of unemployed men-at-arms, accustomed to take what they wanted without regard to human or legal rights; men who had often been the bad characters of their home parishes before they were enrolled in a military contingent.

The older feudalism could no longer supply an adequate fighting force; from the time of Edward I's Welsh wars, other means had been coming into use. Instead of requiring knight service from land-holders, noble lords contracted to supply the king with contingents made up not of their tenants, but of men bound to them by a written indenture and a retaining fee. The system was not confined to the recruiting of armies for France; it permeated fifteenth-century society.

The 'lordship' of those days was a personal relationship based on a cash nexus, lacking the stability of hereditary ties or territorial dependence; in place of the older traditions of faith and loyalty, business methods and frank self-interest dictated social relationships. Not your landlord nor your father's lord, but the man who had made his name in business, war, or politics, was the patron to whom you attached yourself if you were shrewd or ambitious. Even more if you were timorous or defenceless; 'spend somewhat and get yourself a lord, for thereby hang the law and the prophets,' was the advice given to John Paston in 1450; influence was more effective than a good cause if your legal rights were threatened.

It is this bastard feudalism, as it has been called, that is largely responsible for the bad character that true feudalism has acquired in the history books, and it owed its ugliness to the fact that the fief, the landholding, had dropped out of the picture in governmental relationships. The system was parasitic; it flourished by exploiting the non-feudal organs of government. The king's council, the king's exchequer, the king's chancery, the king's law courts were invaded and manipulated by the great men for their own interests. The king's council of these days has been described by Sir John Fortescue. 'When they came together they were so occupied with their own matters and with the matters of their kin, servants, and tenants, that they attended but little to the king's matters, and no matter treated in the council could be kept privy, for the lords told their servants how their causes had sped and who was against them.'

If you had a local dispute, you got your noble patron to see that the judges appointed to look into the matter would be favourable to you. He got at the sheriff to see that the jury was made of your friends; or he intimidated the jury by demonstrating with a band of indentured retainers. It might easily go so far as a raid on your opponent's house; if the local officials had been bribed or intimidated, no one would interfere. 'The law serveth for nought else but to do wrong,' protested the malcontents who followed Jack Cade in 1450.

What of parliament? The fourteenth century had seen the incorporation of the Commons in parliament, and the establishment, as a by-product of the king's military needs, of their strategic position as the body whose consent was requisite for taxation. The fifteenth century is the period in which the forms and traditions of parliaments, and in especial of the Commons, are becoming established. The expression 'the Lower House' comes into use; the Speaker's office is honourable enough for him to figure as one of the signatories of a national manifesto, and his right to control proceedings in the House is fully recognized; the practice of three readings of a bill is mentioned; the bill 'containing in itself the form of an act' replaces the petition which could be garbled in the process of being turned into a statute. The authority of a statute made in parliament is universally recognized as superior to that of any other legislative act.

From the death of Henry V the practice of prorogation is becoming more and more usual, so that the life of a parliament may be prolonged for several sessions. Elections are keenly disputed, and in the counties are marked by canvassing posters and rowdy meetings, so that the famous statute of 1430 is passed to check participation of persons 'of small substance and no worth' by fixing a proper qualification for the voter. New parliamentary boroughs are created; in some instances, undoubtedly, to enable the magnates to get some of their own protégés into the Common House, as a counterweight to the royal servants who are occupying other seats. Statutes are issued in large numbers on ecclesiastical, economic, legal, and police matters; a song of about 1450, however, alludes gloomily to

'Many acts of parliament,
Few kept with true intent.'

The Chief Justice, Sir John Fortescue, whose book *In Praise of the Laws of England* (1470) is the first treatise on the

English constitution, bases a contrast between the absolute monarchy of France and the limited monarchy of England on two facts, firstly, that in England extraordinary taxation needs the consent of parliament, and secondly, that the king cannot make or alter the law of the land without the consent of parliament. But it is clearly on the law itself that, in his eyes, the liberty and security of the common man depends, and for that law to be effective, in the fifteenth as in the twelfth century, the monarchy itself must be strong, and the executive functions of government, which are unquestionably his, must operate effectively.

So Sir John's treatise of 1470, intended to warn his young pupil, the son of Henry VI and Margaret of Anjou, against making French kingship his model, was followed by a discourse exhorting the king of England to strengthen the monarchy by husbanding its economic resources, and by choosing for his councillors expert civil servants rather than selfish magnates who put their own interests first, betrayed the king's interests, and squandered the king's resources. Parliament may be needed for emergency taxation or legislation; for normal government, the king's revenue and king's council and civil servants ought to be self-sufficing.

Poverty of the crown and lack of governance were the crying evils, in the eyes of a shrewd and experienced judge; rectify them, and the good laws of England might provide good justice and good peace for the king's subjects.

But the Wars of the Roses, the Red Rose of Lancaster, and the White Rose of York, dragged on wretchedly. Battle followed battle; and the vanquished were often slain after defeat if they had not fallen in fight. The aristocracy of England seemed to be committing a kind of suicide.

Richard of York, who had earned credit by his upright and capable administration in France and Ireland, and who might have done much for England if Henry's insanity of 1453 had been permanent, induced parliament to accept him as heir-apparent in place of Henry's son in October 1460, but was killed in battle two months later. Richard's son, welcomed by the Londoners as King Edward IV in 1461, defeated the

Lancastrian forces utterly at Towton, and obtained from parliament a full endorsement of his claims as the lawful heir of Richard II.

II

THE BREAKDOWN OF THE MEDIEVAL ECONOMY

It was not only as a political and social system that feudalism was being superseded. Economic forces were cracking the medieval shell, but the new growth was still embryonic, though vigorous enough to add force to the demand for order from a people weary of anarchy and longing for physical security in which to follow up the opportunities opening before them.

The agricultural and pastoral expansion of the thirteenth and fourteenth centuries and the overseas ventures of English merchants and traders had suffered a check in the later fourteenth century, partly through the rivalries of producers and financiers, partly through the devitalizing effects of the Black Death and the recurrent epidemics that followed it, and partly through the self-defeating extravagances of the French wars.

The peasants' rising of 1381, like the labour legislation that helped to provoke it, was evidence of the discomforts, familiar to our generation also, of social adjustment to economic change. The manorial organization of agriculture, like the gild organization of industry, was no longer adequate to the demands of life, labour, and production; but the customs that regulated both techniques and personal rights were difficult to change if interests conflicted.

Slowly and painfully the adjustments were made. New legal relationships of landlord and cultivators were created, new forms of association and organization grew up in industry. The changes in method were accompanied and accelerated by the redistribution of property and wealth resulting from the plague and the wars. Shortage of labour produced a comparatively well-to-do and more mobile labouring class; land changed hands freely as a result of death and speculation; war profiteers, both civil and military, acquired estates. But meantime most of the towns were shrinking in size, the export trade in wool dwindled, lawlessness spilled over from the land to the sea, and piracy in the Channel, though it may have helped to train the fathers of Drake and Hawkins, frustrated the ends of the government's foreign policy.

The total wealth of the country was less; but its redistribution amongst the rising and enterprising classes meant that the very dislocation of society was releasing new energies. The records of the great and growing towns—York, Norwich, Coventry, Bristol, Northampton, and many more—reflect an expansion and a confidence that contrasts markedly with the disorders of the country-side.

By the third quarter of the fifteenth century the potentialities of a general economic revival were visible; a native cloth industry, with something like factory organization, was developing; large areas were being enclosed and thus converted from arable to pasture for the production of the wool demanded by the clothiers. Citizens of other towns besides London welcomed Edward IV with pomp and pageant.

Yorkist rule seemed to promise chances of pursuing profits peacefully. The diplomacy of Edward IV, as of Henry VII later, and the statutes of their parliaments reflect the concern of king, lords, and commons in matters of trade and industry. The crafts, whose management had once been a matter for local municipal authorities, were being regulated and protected by government; overseas trading companies were being recognised; good relations were being established with the great financial and commercial power of Burgundy. Overseas trade had ranged in the days of Canning of Bristol (1399–1474) from Iceland to East Prussia; a new orientation was foreshadowed when Henry VII, in 1496, granted a licence for John Cabot, also of Bristol, to make the famous voyage which issued in the discovery of Nova Scotia.

III
THE RECOVERY OF KINGSHIP, 1461–1509

Edward IV's accession marks the turn of the tide politically as well as economically. The Lancastrians were not finally routed in 1461; Edward's reign was interrupted by two battles in 1464, and a brief restoration of Henry VI for seven months in 1470-71, a 're-adeption' made possible by the defection of Edward's brother, Clarence, and his leading supporter, the 'king-maker' Warwick. None the less, there are clear signs from the first of a firm hand at the helm and a determined attack on corrupt administration.

The policies followed after 1471 seem to have been roughly those which Sir John Fortescue had recommended. But the fatal legacy of blood and treachery was not yet exhausted. Edward had connived at the murder of Henry VI and his son in 1471; the eldest of his two brothers plotted against him a second time and was executed for it in 1478, and on Edward's death in 1483 his younger brother, Richard, who had gained the reputation of an able administrator as Warden of the Scottish Marches, promptly dethroned the young Edward V and made away with him, his brother, and his uncle on the mother's side. When, in 1485, Henry of Richmond, who represented the Beaufort-Lancastrian line through his mother, the widow of a Welsh gentleman called Edmund Tudor, landed in England and defeated and killed Richard III at Bosworth, few contemporaries could have foretold that this was to be the last battle of the Wars of the Roses.

It is true that Henry Tudor strengthened his very weak claim by marrying the daughter of Edward IV, blending the Red and the White Roses, but there were many other descendants of Edward III still alive. Nor were impersonators wanting to urge their claims, supported by the foreign allies and relations of the House of York. But in fact the Tudors had come to stay, and in spite of plots, social and economic upheavals, and the religious revolution, the crown of Henry VII descended in peace to his son and three grandchildren in succession.

It is Shakespeare's plays that afford the best evidence of the impression left on the minds of Englishmen by the thirty years of the Wars of the Roses. Not only in the pictures of sordid treachery, brutality, and human misery drawn in *Henry VI* and *Richard III*, but in the recurrent motif of the horror of anarchy and civil war and the beauty of discipline and order we can trace the unforgotten memories of the days before Tudor rule was established. Fear of the Nemesis that will follow up the deposition and murder of Richard II haunts even the confident Henry V. In Mark Antony's prophecy of the wars to come on Italy after Cæsar's assassination:

'Domestic fury and fierce civil strife . . .
All pity choked by custom of fell deeds,'

we see the ravaged community; in Ulysses' rebuke to the frustrated Greeks in council before Troy, we are shown the fatal results of jealousies and divisions in the very seat of government that should command respect.

'Degree, priority, and place,
Insisture, cause, proportion, season, form,
Office and custom, in all line of order'

on these, so the Tudor citizen holds, depend the well-being of the community, learning, commerce, national prestige; without them 'The enterprise is sick.'

Feudalism, for all its insistence on priority and place, had proved inadequate for the needs of government, however much its traditions of deference and responsibility might linger in the English social system. The oligarchy, unworthy of the name of aristocracy, had cut their own throat; the handful of lay lords in Henry's first parliament carried little weight. All men, consciously or unconsciously, looked to the monarchy for salvation, not to supersede or override the common law, but to enforce it. The king must be strong; and if he needed to sharpen old tools for the purpose they were ready to approve. The preamble of Henry VII's famous act of 1487 enumerated the various ways by which the over mighty subject had made the jury system valueless and the laws of the land to be of little effect. The committee of council that made use of established prerogative techniques for the enforcement of those laws, though it came to have an evil reputation as the hated Star Chamber in the days of Archbishop Laud, was regarded as a radiant centre of justice under the Tudors. Public order was the ally of private men's rights in the public eyes. It was to king rather than to parliament that the Englishman looked to safeguard his liberties in the early sixteenth century.

Henry VII, seen from the standpoint of later history, may seem the herald of a new age: 'The politic governance of Henry VII' was to be the forerunner of 'The triumphant reign of Henry VIII.' In fact, none of the devices that he used was an innovation. Neither the conception of the king as the fountain of justice and the guardian of order, nor the employment of 'new men' in preference to aristocrats in official posts, nor the use of judicial methods outside the ordinary course of the common law were unknown in medieval times. Equitable jurisdiction was no new thing in Chancery: Henry merely extended its use.

He actually revived the old *quo warranto* procedure of Edward I and, like Edward IV, asserted his financial rights as feudal overlord. The agents on whom he relied for local government were those justices of the peace whose functions had been defined in the parliaments of Edward III; his use of the Household for his successful financial administration had been anticipated by the Plantagenets and by Edward IV. His parliaments, with a preponderantly ecclesiastical House of Lords, met at long intervals, the Commons being effectively managed by Speakers who, like those of Edward IV and Richard III, were royal officials. It is his skilful exploitation of the situation that he found, and his genius for acquiring, husbanding, and enlarging the revenues which are the first requisite for a strong monarchy, that marks him out as the canniest of English kings and explains his success as a ruler.

But in his attitudes and assumptions Henry VII belongs to the Middle Ages. Above all, he, like his mother, the Lady Margaret Beaufort, was a devout servant of the Church, continuing the benefactions of Henry VI. The chapel in Westminster Abbey where Henry lies with his wife and mother ranks with that of King's College, Cambridge, completed by him and his son, as the supreme achievements of the last phase of Gothic architecture; that so-called perpendicular style which is to be found in England alone. The decorations of Henry's tomb are Renaissance work; the structure of the chapel is medieval.

CHAPTER XIV

THE UNIFICATION OF THE NATIONAL LANGUAGE

WHETHER we use the medieval expression 'community of the realm' or the modern word 'nation,' the body that has a common political consciousness requires a common tongue. Alfred's work had opened the way to a common English language that could be used for religion, business, and government, though clerics had to be bilingual if they were to keep contact with Europe. But the Norman Conquest meant the introduction of a new tongue. For centuries after 1066 the ruling class used French for social intercourse and personal correspondence. For all formal and official correspondence, for legal records, for keeping accounts, whether of the state or of estates, and for all literary, scientific, philosophical, or ecclesiastical writing, Latin was the language.

It was said in the twelfth century that French was the tongue understood by the great, the middle, and the lower classes, but the English tongue was also in use by the cultured as well as the illiterate. The Anglo-Saxon chronicle was kept up at Peterborough till 1154, and other histories were written in English under Richard and John. Women in all probability helped to link the languages. They must have talked French to their husbands and English to their servants, and their ignorance of Latin led to the writing of religious works for them in English.

One of these, the charming *Rule for Anchoresses*, was widely read for at least three centuries. The best pastors of the twelfth century, like Abbot Samson of Bury St. Edmunds in the days of Henry II, preached in English. A writer with a sense of the past, like William of Malmesbury in Stephen's days, made use of Anglo-Saxon works in composing his *History of the Kings of England*. Clerks and bailiffs needed to be trilingual, having

161

to handle English-speaking peasants, keep records in Latin, and report to their masters in French. Stephen Langton preached in English, lectured in Latin, and wrote letters in French. Polite literature, romances, lays, and satires were in French; ballads and proverbs survived, mainly orally, in English.

But a witty and sophisticated English poem, contrasting the life of the scholar with that of the man of the world, survives from the opening years of the thirteenth century, and in the reign of Henry III English is beginning to be a political language. Henry III's proclamation to the people of England was translated into English as well as French, and Magna Carta was read in English in the shire courts to reach those who had no French; whilst the popular satirist, who ridiculed the ignoble part played by Henry III's brother at the battle of Lewes, labelled him 'Richard the Trichard' in a racy English ballad, and Edward I's subjects boasted of the exploits of 'him with the Long shanks' over the recreant Scots.

Robert of Gloucester's contemporary rhymed history of the Barons' Wars was written in English, and the translation of Langtoft's French chronicle into English early in the fourteenth century shows that the use of English was spreading upwards. Froissart says that when the Hundred Years' War began parliament ordered all lords, knights, and townsmen to *teach* their children French, as it would be useful in the war. He also relates how a clerk skilled in the three tongues rose before the king and the whole parliament and spoke in English, 'that all might understand him,' for, as an English contemporary wrote:

> 'Learned, unlearned, old and young,
> All understand the English tongue.'

Edward III spoke English on occasion, and it seems probable that it was Richard II's mother tongue. Letters, both official and unofficial, were still in French, but courtly poets wrote in both languages, and Chaucer and Langland had a wide public for their English poems, to judge by the manuscripts surviving. If the *Canterbury Tales* introduce us to the English on holiday, *Piers Plowman*, *Richard the Redeless*, and *Mum Sothsegger* put us in direct touch once more with the politically conscious, as they tell of those who serve the king 'in Chequer and Chancery,' and stress the responsibilities of all orders of society from the ploughman to the king, whom 'might of the commons made to reign.'

In the poem written in the midst of the revolution of 1399, Richard II, as 'uncounselled' as his far distant ancestor Ethelred, is told that he has thrown away the crown of love and loyalty that he had inherited as a child, 'before he knew himself.' 'Repent yourself, Richard the Redeless, you that led your life and ruled your people lawless! Allegiance standeth not by pleasing of princes, or tallage of towns or ruthless routs, but by leading of law, well tempered by love.' But the satirist does not stop here. He turns on the members of parliament and tells them their duty. 'They are the servants of those who send them, and if they are false to the men of the shires who pay their wages, they are not worthy of their hire.' And again: 'When knights have come to the parliament for the commons, they should not spare their speech lest they bring home a bagful of unhealed sores.' The different types of member in the chapter house at Westminster are hit off in language that is not entirely out of date to-day:

'Some sat there like a nought in arithmetic, that marks a place, but has no value in itself. Some had taken bribes, so that the shire they represented had no advantage from their presence in parliament. Some were tattlers, who went to the king and warned him against men who were really his good friends. Some slumbered and slept and said little. Some stammered and mumbled and did not know what they meant to say. Some were afraid to take any step without their master's orders. Some were so pompous and dull-witted that they were hopelessly involved before they reached the end of their speeches, and no one could make out what they wanted to say. And some of them dashed ahead so recklessly that they had to be warned to keep to subjects which were their own business and which they understood. Some went with the majority whichever way they went, while some would not commit themselves; and some were so afraid of great men that they forsook righteousness.'

The rising of 1381 had been heralded by English verses that passed from mouth to mouth:

> Jack the Miller hath ground small, small,
> The king's son of Heaven shall pay for it all.

Political ballads and songs have come down to us echoing less passionately the voice of the crowd.

> To know if parliament be wise
> Look to the common loss or gain,
> The kingdom's weal in the commons lies
> And likewise all the kingdom's bane.
> Lords never know the commons' griefs
> Until their rents begin to cease.

This invasion of political life by the English language can be explained in part, as we saw, by the growing importance of the English-speaking orders of society, but also by the antagonism to foreigners that becomes vocal under Henry III, and is directed alike against the Poitevins and Provençals in the king's employ, and the aliens who obtain English benefices from the pope. The anti-French feeling roused by the Hundred Years' War further accelerated the adoption of English for general purposes. Three years after Crecy, a leading schoolmaster set the fashion of making his pupils construe in English instead of French, and it soon became general. In 1362 it was provided that cases in the law courts should be pleaded in English, not French. In 1399 Henry of Lancaster put forward his claim to the throne in English, in Westminster Hall, and it was in English that the estates of the realm rendered up their homage and fealty to Richard II at the Tower, whereas their predecessors had made their 'defiance' of Edward II at Kenilworth in 1327 in French.

For English to become the national language some outcome of the war of local dialects had to be reached. The victory of the midland dialect is probably attributable to the predominance of London, which in the course of the fourteenth century had come to be not merely the commercial but the governmental metropolis of England.

This was due not so much to the Tower in the East as to the Palace in the West. From the days of Henry II, when the first articulate exchequer clerk sat at his window looking on the Thames, to the days when Edward I held his coronation feast in Westminster Hall, and Edward III sent the knights of the shire to discuss grants with the burgesses in the Painted Chamber, and his workmen decorated the Council Chamber with a starred ceiling, Westminster was the centre for government offices. The staple for wool was placed there in 1353.

In the thirteenth and early fourteenth centuries, about half the parliaments met at Westminster; in the last forty years of Edward III's reign, only one parliament was held elsewhere. London, 'the flower of cities all,' was the focus of governmental activity, and in the fifteenth century its law schools made it almost a third university for the education of young gentlemen. It was natural that London speech should set the standard for national speech.

And it is a London document that records what may almost be called the official abandonment of the French language, which was a by-product of the renewal of the Hundred Years War by Henry V. His despatches from France were written in English, and the citizens of London, led by the Brewers' Company, took his example to heart. 'Whereas our mother tongue hath in modern days begun to be honorably enlarged . . . and our most excellent King Henry hath procured the common idiom to be recommended by the exercise of writing, and the greater part of the lords and commons have begun to make their matters to be noted down in our mother tongue,' therefore, they say, the ordinances of their craft are to be written in English. The same was happening with the City chronicles. In the thirteenth century the chronicle of the mayors and sheriffs had been kept in Latin, in the fourteenth century in French, but in the fifteenth century it was in English that civic events were recorded and the rejoicings over the victory of Agincourt described:

'On the 29th of October, when the new mayor should ride

and take his charge at Westminster, came tidings to London while men were in their beds that the king had fought and had the battle and the field aforesaid. And anon as they had tidings thereof they went to all the churches in the city of London and rang all the bells of every church, and solemnly all the priests of every church and other men that were lettered sang *Te Deum Laudamus*.

'And against nine of the bell were warned all the orders of religious men of the city of London to go a procession from St. Paul's to St. Edward's Shrine at Westminster, and the new mayor and his aldermen with all the crafts of London also went from St. Paul's to Westminster, and offered at St. Edward's Shrine before the mayor took his charge. And when the mayor had taken his charge every man came riding home from Westminster, and they were joyful and glad, and thanked our Lord Jesus Christ and his mother St. Mary, and St. George, and all the holy company of Heaven and said: "This is the day which the Lord hath made.' "

London was not alone; all over England the towns were beginning to keep their chronicles and records in the mother tongue. English was becoming the business language.

And, as the London Brewers had observed, it was becoming the official language of parliament, whose records, kept in French and Latin in the fourteenth century, contain more and more English entries—petitions, grants by the commons, Richard of York's claim to the crown in 1460, the long and elaborate statement by the commons in 1461 of Edward IV's primogenitive right and the usurpation of the Lancastrians, and, finally, the whole record. The Privy Seal and Signet letters ceased to be written in French, as did Bills in Chancery. French was becoming a foreign language, and the kings were beginning to employ a special French secretary for their foreign correspondence.

The English language itself, 'honorably enlarged' by the increased incorporation of many French words, and made supple by the genius of Chaucer, who was equally at home in a courtly, an official, or a popular environment, was coming to serve the most manifold uses. It was probably the clerk of the council who in 1436 addressed to the lords of the council a remarkable pamphlet in verse, *The Libel of English Policy*, urging with a mass of detailed evidence a well-sustained argument in favour of terminating the wasteful and unproductive war with France, and concentrating on a good merchant navy and the development of English commerce. It is the first impassioned dissertation on the theme 'Look to your moat.'

'Cherish merchandise, keep the admiralty,
That we be masters of the narrow sea.'

As he sets forth the technicalities of trade, so those of theology are expounded by Wyclif and Peacock, and those of government and law by Sir John Fortescue, whilst the emotional and picturesque potentialities of the language are being developed in Malory's great romances. Copies of *The Brut*, that popular version of British history from the fall of Troy to the present day which was continually being added to by different writers as the fifteenth century advanced, were being multiplied for sale to a growing circle of readers, with other chronicles in prose and verse; a common tradition of national history was being established, later to be transformed by Hall and immortalized by Shakespeare.

But to the reader who desires acquaintance with the ordinary man and woman, its use for ordinary purposes is even more illuminating in the fifteenth century, as more and more schools were founded, and more and more lay folk were writing as well as reading English. In the thirteenth century the literate knight had been noteworthy; now not only the squire and the burgess, but the squire's wife and the burgess's daughter were writing or dictating letters and memoirs. In the familiar letters of the Stonor and Paston families, in the meditations of Julian of Norwich, in the racy autobiography of Margery Kempe of King's Lynn, we make a first-hand contact with medieval men and women in a language recognizably our own.

When a wife writes to her husband: 'Rather break up the household than take sojournants (paying guests); servants be not so diligent as they were wont to be'; when a country gentleman writes to an absentee landlord: 'As I walk in my recreation, I may see that in your woods your farmer hath made great waste and destruction, the which should cause a great displeasure to me if it were done in my woods'; or a son writes to his father: 'I send you home Peacock again. He is not for me. God send grace that he may do you good service, which is not likely'; or the schoolboy asks that he may 'come and sport him at London a day or two this term time' with his brother; when the parliamentary candidate discusses his chances of election with his agent, or the pilgrim tells us how she was 'bitten and stung full evil, both day and night, through communing with a company of poor folk' on her journey through Germany, or the soldier writes from France: 'Pray for us that we may come soon out of this unlusty soldier's life into the life of England,' we achieve an intimacy with the past unattainable in times when only the great and the learned wrote, and that in a language other than the one they used colloquially.

The girl who begs her lover that her letter 'be not seen of none earthly creature save only yourself' is far removed from the noble correspondents of earlier days, whose letters, dictated and translated, passed through so many hands that the most intimate and important parts of the message were always conveyed orally through the bearer. Only through his own writings can we really know a man of the past; few medieval kings of England are as near to us as Alfred the Great, and few laymen as familiar as those clerics to whom Latin was a living language.

Under Edward IV the printing press came to accelerate the process of unification and assimilation and to quicken national consciousness. By the end of the fifteenth century the English tongue was an instrument ready to respond to the demands of historians like Hall, whose chronicle created 'the Tudor historical myth'; of lyricists and satirists like Wyatt and Skelton; of educationists like Colet and Elyot; of biographers like More and Roper; of religious controversialists like Tyndale; of preachers and liturgists like Latimer and Cranmer. Sixteenth-century England could speak for herself, to the world and to posterity.

CHAPTER XV

THE REFORMATION: ENGLAND STANDS ALONE

1529–1558

In the long process of evolution by which medieval England became modern England, the monarchy had won the last round. Aristocracy had been unable to deliver the goods, and had, in effect, handed back the job of government to the rulers. The middling orders were more than content that it should be so, and the Tudors were bending their energies to the task of steering the nation through a period of social, economic, and intellectual revolution such as western civilization had never known before. The new learning, the new prices, the new world, the new theology were making their impact on the English commonwealth. The kings of England, unlike their contemporaries in Europe, found that to meet this challenge they had no need to abandon the tools of government that had been forged in the Middle Ages. It is true that the local liberties of up-country palatinates and lordships and the rivalries of jealous boroughs had to be subdued and their separatism merged in the national consciousness, but the king's council and parliament, the common law courts, the equitable jurisdiction of the chancery and the justices of the peace all proved adaptable to the needs of the sixteenth and seventeenth centuries. They could serve the purposes of rulers who accepted responsibility, not only for the safety and order, but also for the material well-being and social equipoise of the whole community.

The identification of the ruler with the nation, expressing itself alike in the outrageous elaborations of the law of treason under Henry VIII, and the extravagances of Gloriana-worship under Elizabeth, was based on a sense of the realities and

169

dangers of those days. To sixteenth-century Englishmen, the prince was indeed 'the life, the head, and the authority of all things that be done in the realm of England.'

For this identification of king and nation to be complete, however, one link with the medieval world had to be broken. Sovereignty was a conception unknown to medieval political thought, because the only recognized sovereign was God; and the rulers of the world, whether in Church or State, were his deputies, with distinct functions and distinct spheres of action. In the sphere of faith and morals the effective authority of the Church was unquestioned; all recognized its jurisdiction in matters of ecclesiastical discipline, in the matrimonial concerns of laymen, in cases of heresy, immorality, sacrilege, blasphemy, or perjury.

The canon law, built up by the judgments and decrees of popes and councils, and administered in the courts of English archdeacons, bishops, and judges delegate, linked ever more and more closely with the supreme tribunal at Rome, was part of the everyday order of things. All laymen, in theory at least, were equally subject to this spiritual jurisdiction.

As the Emperor Theodosius had had to submit to the discipline of Ambrose, so William the Conqueror had had to seek remission for his irregular marriage; so Henry II had had to do penance for the murder caused by his violent speech; so John had had to seek release from excommunication for his refusal to accept a papal judgment. And, conversely, the popes had recognized the right of the feudal suzerain to claim counsel, service, and dues from the prelates who held baronies of the crown, and had advised the chapters who elected bishops to choose not saintly recluses, but experienced men fitted to serve God in the state as well as the Church.

Without the help of such men, indeed, in the centuries when literacy was still rare, the kings of England could never have built up the governmental system which made the kingdom one. Roger of Salisbury and his great-nephew who wrote the *Dialogue of the Exchequer* were the first of a long line of churchmen who presided over the royal treasury; and save for a short period in the fourteenth century, every chancellor was an ecclesiastic until Wolsey fell in 1529, the year that marked the end of medieval England. To the popes, as to Richard Fitz Neal, it seemed right that the Church should serve the community by helping to secure peace and order and to maintain the material resources of the crown.

The monarchy was the means by which justice with mercy could be exercised, the rights of the Church upheld, and the weak protected. In theory the partnership was ideal; in practice it was not always possible to draw a hard and fast line between sin and crime; between the alms of the faithful and the mammon of unrighteousness; between spiritual freedom and lawlessness; between peace and the condonation of evil; in a word, between the spiritual and the temporal spheres of action.

Before the Norman Conquest no serious difficulty had appeared, but William I's application of continental ecclesiastical standards in England began the process by which English clergy became conscious of a double loyalty, and English laity made direct contact with a foreign tribunal. When the resistance of the first three Norman kings to the pull of Rome was relaxed under Stephen, the 'liberty of the English Church' came to mean freedom of access to Rome, and the recognition that it was 'that part of the Western Church which the Most High had planted in England.'

It was this consciousness of community which Henry II roused when, in his quarrel with the heroic but provocative Thomas of Canterbury, he asserted the rights of the secular law over the persons of the clerical order and had, in the event, to admit both the privileged position of the clerical criminal and the authority of the pope to interpret canon law for English litigants, a right which, as John found, involved adjudication on disputed ecclesiastical elections.

But there still remained the inescapable problem of the maintenance of the ministers of things spiritual. They had to be fed and clothed, and from time immemorial lands and rights to gifts had constituted the 'livings' of the clergy. Secular law and police were required to establish the right to such property and to secure it against violence; and the king's justice and the common law courts offered far and away the best security.

Whatever Rome might suggest, and however much the Church courts might seek to extend their jurisdiction, clerical land-owners in England preferred to vindicate their rights to land in the king's courts, and the lay patrons, who took a pro-prietary interest in the churches and abbeys founded by their ancestors, followed a similar course.

It was through this gap in the defences of the Church that the lay power extended its sway over churchmen. The Church, in return, extended her demands, and the popes, assailed by petitioners for preferment, based upon the doctrine of plenitude of power a claim to control temporalities as well as spiritualities, to supersede the rights of native electors and native patrons, and not only to tax the English clergy for the financing of papal foreign policy, but to forbid their taxation by the king for the defence of the realm.

Henry III and Edward I, both devout Christians and both owing much to the conciliatory offices of great papal legates, found themselves at issue with the papacy over taxation and clerical appointments. Neither they nor their clergy could deny the authority the exercise of which they resented, nor could the popes with impunity push their claims to extremes. But when the lesser popes and lesser kings of the fourteenth century reached a working compromise whereby the English clergy were supposed freely to grant the taxes which the king had no right to demand, and came to a tacit agreement to override the rights of native patrons and chapters, the inde-pendence of the Church in England was, in fact, undermined.

Bishoprics, archdeaconries, and canonries came to be regarded more and more as constituting a fund from which the salaries of ministers of state and civil servants should be paid, the actual work being done by an underpaid deputy. Saints and scholars might now and then obtain preferment, but the politician or government clerk was the commoner type. Something of the deterioration in political life in the later Middle Ages may be attributed to the replacement of prelates like Anselm, Stephen Langton, Edmund Rich, or Grosseteste by men like Walter Reynolds and John Stratford, who assisted in the deposition of Edward II; William of Wykeham, the adherent of Edward III's mistress, Alice Perrers; or Arundel, who presided over the downfall of Richard II.

The divisions of Christendom in the fifteenth century and the dying down of the monastic impulse further weakened the hold of ecclesiastical institutions on men's loyalty. Religious devotion was expressing itself in individual rather than social forms; not only in the intellectual and moral questionings of Wyclif and his school, but in the mystical and devotional writings of contemplatives like Richard Rolle, Walter Hilton, Julian of Norwich, and the author of *The Cloud of Unknowing*.

Protests against papal doctrine and clerical wealth were driven underground by persecution, the orthodox Henry IV and Henry V lending the arm of the state to burn the heretics whom the Church convicted, but they persisted; and on the eve of the Protestant revolution the most devout of the orthodox, men like Fisher and Sir Thomas More, were acutely aware of the need for reformation in the Church. They differed from the average English churchman, however, in seeing clearly the remoter implications of a repudiation of papal supremacy.

In England, unlike Germany, France, or Scotland, the revolt against Rome was led by the monarch. To the thrifty, politic, and orthodox Henry VII succeeded in 1509 the magnificent young athlete, scholar, musician, and theologian Henry VIII, eager to try his hand at the game of international politics, hardly yet aware of the resources at his disposal, but determined to have his own way.

> 'For my pastance,
> Hunt, song, and dance,
> My heart is set!
> *Who shall me let?*'

More warned Thomas Cromwell, his successor as first minister to Henry, as More himself had succeeded Wolsey, of the dangers of serving a lion's cub. 'If a lion knew his own strength, hard were it for any man to rule him.'

The material wealth and established system of government that his father's precedence had secured to him; the goodwill earned for the monarchy by twenty-four years of growing order and security; the rapid advancement of national consciousness by the new vehicle of communication, the printed word; the growing recognition of the potentialities of English skill, of English land, and of the English tongue, all were behind the great onward wave on which the new king rode triumphantly.

From the thrilling game of the balance of power, played with the young rulers of France and the empire, Henry turned, after some eighteen years, to problems nearer home. By the Spanish wife, his brother's widow, whom he had married on his accession, he had only one daughter. Whether moved by conscience, by concern for the succession, or by desire, he sought a divorce. To secure an heir, he must have the law on his side, and Rome, the only legal authority, proved impossible to manipulate.

The jurisdiction of the pope over matrimonial causes had to be repudiated and, to buttress the new assertion of monarchic powers, the half-sleeping institution of parliament had to be reawakened,[1] to frame the statute law that all England acknowledged as good, and to let the voice of the new nobility and the substantial merchants and gentry be heard.

On 3rd November, 1529, the parliament met that was to break all precedents; to last for seven years; to cut the financial and judicial ties between the English Church and Rome; to reject the pope's ecclesiastical authority; and to declare the king Supreme Head on earth of the Church of England, recognizing his disciplinary powers in matters of faith and morals; and to exemplify this by dissolving the monasteries which Henry's inspectors reported as unfit, and transferring their property to the king.

These seven years saw England's transition from the medieval to the modern world. The Reformation Parliament, by substituting the Church of England for the Church in England, declared the realm to be self-sufficient for

[1] In the forty-four years since Henry VII's accession, only ten parliaments had met, sitting altogether for twenty-eight months. Between November 1529 and March 1536 parliament sat for sixteen months.

ecclesiastical as well as political purposes. But in denying the right of any external authority to lay down law that must be obeyed in England, in claiming supremacy in all causes ecclesiastical as well as temporal within his dominions, Henry had, all unawares, raised up a rival to his own powers.

When More, who was a lawyer as well as a saint, denied the validity of a statute that overrode the law of God by substituting king for pope, he was repudiating the doctrine not of an absolute king but of a sovereign parliament. In using it to achieve his will, Henry had re-created parliament; he had opened the way for that alliance of puritanism and the House of Commons that was, under the Stuarts, to defeat the new theology of divine right and the new politics of absolutism.

Henry VIII, who had earned the title of Defender of the Faith by a treatise against Luther's doctrines, had no intention of changing the theological basis of the faith of the English Church. This fact, with the long period of compromise in the preceding centuries, probably accounts for the ready acceptance by most leading churchmen of the new situation. Gardiner, to whom it seemed a matter of politics rather than creed, was more typical than Fisher, who died with More sooner than acknowledge the king as head of the Church.

But Henry, after asserting himself as the champion of orthodoxy by his act 'for abolishing diversities of opinions' in 1539, found himself drifting towards alliance with the Protestants, who were growing more hopeful as their cause advanced on the Continent, and before the end of his reign he had not only permitted an English Bible to be placed in the churches, but had sanctioned the use of 'prayers and suffrages in our native English tongue.'

The flood gates were open, and when he died in 1547 the council that governed in the name of his nine-year-old son Edward VI pushed ahead with the work of eliminating both the forms and the doctrines of the old religion. The country folk of the west revolted against the new Prayer Book, as those of the north had risen in protest against the dissolution of the monasteries, but London and the more populous and wealthy south-eastern counties, in close touch with the Continent, supported the destruction of images and the simplification of ritual. The positive and priceless achievement of the reign was the *Book of Common Prayer*, largely the work of Archbishop Cranmer, a Cambridge theologian who had risen to prominence by helping Henry to legalize his marriage with Anne Boleyn.

The Prayer Book, with its rendering of the ancient Latin prayers in noble English and its retention of much of the old order of worship, preserved continuity with the Catholic Church of the Middle Ages; it was to be the nurse of the severed Christian community; to win its love and focus its loyalty. And, by the greatest good fortune, the substitution of the vernacular for the Latin liturgy did not break the tradition of English Church music. Tallis and Merbecke[1] seconded Cranmer's work in bridging the transition from the Roman to the Anglican services, and keeping intact the living chain of song that links the worshippers in an English cathedral to-day with those of the past.

But there were ugly features in Edwardian Protestantism. The fanaticism of the iconoclastic mobs was matched by the greed and selfishness of the council, who carried Henry VIII's policy of confiscation further by dissolving nearly all religious associations and annexing their property, including the endowments of many schools. The colleges of Oxford and Cambridge barely escaped, and the Lords defeated the attempt of the Commons to re-found the plundered schools, a measure that might have given England educational advantages equal to those later bestowed on Scotland by the reformed religion.

A repressive social policy and their own internal disputes further lowered the standing of the council, and on the death of Edward, a precocious boy who supported the new faith cold-bloodedly, his Catholic sister Mary succeeded easily in defeating an attempt to foist her Protestant cousin Lady Jane Grey on the country. Unhappy alike in her birth and her marriage, the girl usurper made a good Christian end at the block, and Mary, with equally sincere religious convictions, addressed herself to the task of undoing her father's work.

[1] John Merbecke, organist at St. George's Chapel, Windsor, composed the settings for the services in the Prayer Book of 1549.

Mary Tudor belonged to the past. She inherited the rigidity as well as the religious devotion of her Spanish mother, intensified by the twenty years of repression that had followed the nullification of that mother's marriage, and the bastardization of herself at the age of seventeen. To bring back England, which welcomed her enthusiastically, into the bosom of the Catholic Church, was a high mission; to seek support in this project by marrying her Catholic cousin, Philip of Spain, seemed an obvious policy.

It proved fatal, both to her cause and to her personal happiness. England was officially reconciled to Rome; all anti-papal legislation was repealed, and dissent from the old faith dealt with by methods becoming painfully familiar to a distracted Europe. Close on three hundred obstinate Protestants, ranging from working men to the archbishop, who redeemed a record of academic hedging by his humble and courageous end, were convicted in the Church courts and burnt as heretics. But Mary could not restore to the Church the lands taken from the monasteries; land speculators or members of the new nobility had bought them from the crown, and property rights must be respected.

The attempt to burn out Protestantism proved that the new religion was more than 'an affair of statute.' From the first, the executions evoked passionate sympathy for the sufferers, waverers were strengthened by their faithfulness, and Mary's persistence in the attempt to re-convert England awakened hatred for her cause and herself. Her eager hopes of a child were disappointed, and her Spanish husband, having drawn England into war with her old enemy France, abandoned his plain middle-aged wife in her sickness to pursue more absorbing concerns elsewhere.

The French capture of Calais, the last remnant of Edward III's conquests, was the final blow. On 17th November 1558 the most honest of the Tudors died defeated and broken-hearted, and England 'made merry for the new queen,' the child of Anne Boleyn, the twenty-five-year-old Elizabeth. The state Church, with the parliamentary monarchy that created it, had come to stay.

CONCLUSION

THE Englishman of Elizabeth I's day, confronted by hazards and opportunities unknown to his ancestors, owed those ancestors more, perhaps, than he was willing to recognize. The fields on to which he turned his sheep had been won from the woodlands and brought under the plough by centuries of labour, as the kerseys, russets, and worsteds that he exported to Europe were the product of the experience of generations of sheep-farming ancestors, and of skills acquired by spinners, weavers, and fullers from the days of Offa to those of Jack of Newbury. The churches, whose graven and stained images he was carelessly destroying, enshrined traditions of devotion, symbolism, and craftsmanship stretching back from Henry VII through William of Wykeham, Henry III, and Edward the Confessor to Dunstan and Benedict Biscop; as the forms of that worship, and the prayers he used in them carried over to the new age a large measure of the dignity and beauty of the old order. When he and his friends sat down to a sociable evening's singing, the madrigals in which they intertwined their voices embodied a musical tradition going back beyond the great Dunstable, who composed the Agincourt song, 'Our King went forth to Normandy,' and who 'spread the sweet arts of music throughout the world,' to the unknown monk who noted down, 'Sumer is i-cumen in' in the days of Henry III; even to English singers as remote as Alfred and Caedmon. The ships in which he set out to explore a new world had been evolved by centuries of trial and error through Edward III's galleys, from the long ships of Cnut and Alfred and the unknown vessels in which Hengist and Horsa crossed the North Sea; as the mariner's compass which he used derived from the experiments and discoveries of medieval ship-men and scientists. The great towns, whose aldermen in their scarlet gowns welcomed him on his return from his voyage of discovery, looked back through a long vista of civic activity and

178

commercial enterprise to the painfully acquired charters that had given them at once their liberties and their place in the community of the realm, and beyond that, to the Norman castle, the Danish or Roman trading station, or the Anglo-Saxon market town from which they sprang.

The country gentleman who met his fellow justices of the peace at quarter sessions, and took anxious thought for the manners and morals, the well-being and the safety of his own village, was heir to the traditions not only of the knights who fought at Crecy, but of the suitors of the shire court who had stood up to the king's sheriff under Henry III and who had reported the customs of their shire to William the Conqueror; of the thegns who upheld the rights of their neighbours in the shire moots of Cnut's and Edgar's day; and even of those far-distant Angles and Saxons who had agreed amongst themselves in the primitive local assemblies of the Heptarchy how the burden of royal tribute should be distributed.

The new nobility, building the country houses that were to glorify Tudor England, inherited from the earls and barons of the high Middle Ages not only their titles but their established place in the polity as royal councillors and legislators, together with that sense of personal responsibility both to superiors and inferiors which was the permanent legacy of feudalism to English political life. The clerks of exchequer and chancery had no need to look abroad for 'the new Italian invention of administrative efficiency'; they used the formulas and filing systems and preserved the pride of honourable service transmitted to them from the days of Ranulf Glanvill and Richard Fitz Neal.

Most precious of all, in the common law of England the great lawyers of the fifteenth and sixteenth centuries—Lyttelton, Sir Robert Rede, Antony FitzHerbert—were guarding and burnishing armour forged in the Middle Ages; armour which, though scorned by enlightened young humanists as 'barbarous and less convenient to the order of nature than the Roman laws,' was in the next generation to be the first defence of English liberties against the encroachments of the New Monarchy.

CHRONOLOGICAL TABLE

CHRONOLOGICAL TABLE

KINGS AND GREAT MEN	GOVERNMENT	RELIGION
BC Cymbeline king of Catuvellauni		
AD	Britain a Roman Province till 410 61 Boadicea's rising	
100	121 Hadrian's Wall marks northern limit of effective Roman rule	
200		
300		
400 "Arthur" of Britain Aelle of Sussex (1st 'Bretwealda')	410 Romans disown responsibility for Britain	429 } Visits of St. Germanus 447 } ca. 450 Settlement in Britain of Angles and Saxons begins
500 560-84 Ceawlin of Wessex (2nd 'Bretwealda') 560-616 Ethelbert of Kent (3rd 'Bretwealda')		597 Roman Mission to Kent
600 600 Raedwald of E. Anglia (4th 'Bretwealda') 616-32 Edwin of Northumbria (5th 'Bretwealda') 633-41 Oswald of Northumbria (6th 'Bretwealda') 641-70 Oswin of Northumbria (7th 'Bretwealda')	Laws of Ethelbert of Kent	627 Roman mission to Northumbria 632 Flight of Roman missionaries 634 Celtic Mission from Iona: Lindisfarne founded 635 Conversion of Wessex begins Conversion of East Anglia by Felix 664 Roman use accepted for Northumbria at Whitby 668-90 Theodore organizes English Church 681 Wilfrid converts Sussex
700 Offa	688 Laws of Ine of Wessex	Willibrord in Frisia to 739 718-54 Boniface evangelizing Germany

Vertical annotations spanning the 600–700 section: (Aidan to 651) · Hilda of Whitby 614-680 · (Bede 674-735) · Mercian Supremacy

CHRONOLOGICAL TABLE

ART AND LETTERS	COMMERCE AND INDUSTRY	EXTERNAL RELATIONS
		BC
	Foundation of Verulam and Camulodunum	75 Coming of Belgae
		55 Caesar's invasion
		AD
	Foundation of London Road system laid down	43 Invasion of Claudius
		100
		200
	Contraction of towns and	275 Saxon raids on Britain beginning
	Wider development of villa life in country	300
		350 Picts and Scots raiding Britain
		400
ca. 540 Gildas' *Destruction of Britain*		500
		571 Saxons reach Severn
		600
		613 Northumbrian Angles reach Irish Sea
674-89 Foundation by Benedict Biscop of Wearmouth and Jarrow, with library stocked by books from Rome Caedmon (dies 680)		
		690 West Saxons reach Exeter
		700
731 Bede's *Ecclesiastical History* 782-804 Alcuin of York teaching at Court of Charlemagne.	Standard silver penny currency established by Offa 796 Commercial treaty between Offa and Charlemagne	Construction of Offa' Dyke between Wales and Mercia 793-4 Danes sack Lindisfarne and Jarrow

The Carved Crosses of Northumbria

KINGS AND GREAT MEN	GOVERNMENT	RELIGION
800		
802-39 Egbert of Wessex		Wholesale destruction of monasteries and churches by Danes
871-99 Alfred	878 After victory at Edington Alfred ruler of W. Mercia: and after 886, of London	
899-925 Edward	*ca.* 890 Alfred's *Laws*	
900	909 ⎰ Reconquest of Dane-	Conversion of Danelaw to Christianity
925-40 Athelstan	law; Midlands organ- ized in shires and hun- dreds, under aldermen and reeves	
959-75 Edgar	to Regulations against thieves by London peace-gild, and by Edgar's ordinance of the 975 ⎱ Hundred	Revival of monasticism 960 Dunstan Archbishop of Canterbury to Oswald at Worcester 992 Aethelwold at Win- chester *Regularis Concordia*
979-1016 Ethelred	973 Coronation of Edgar, with oath and unction, at Bath	
1000		1012 Murder of Archbishop Alphege by Danes
1013 Swein.		
1016-35 Cnut	Many grants of royal privileges to abbeys and great laymen	
1042 Edward the Confessor		1052 Newly appointed Nor- man archbishop driven out; Stigand replaces him at Canterbury
1066 (Jan.) Harold Dec. 25) William I	1066-72 Introduction of ten- ure by knight service 1074 Revolt of three earls put down	1070 Lanfranc appointed arch- bishop in place of Stigand, deposed with other irreg- ularly appointed bishops at council of Winchester, by papal authority 1072 Spiritual cases withdrawn from jurisdiction of lay courts
1087 William II	1086 The Domesday inquiry 1088 Baronial revolts sup- and pressed 1095	Cluniac and other new mona- steries founded

(Dunstan 910-88 — marginal note alongside 900–979 section)

Art and Letters	Commerce and Industry	External Relations
		800
ca. 890-99 Alfred's English works 893 Asser's *Life of Alfred* Anglo-Saxon Chronicle kept up in various monasteries		835 Danes land in Sheppey 855 Danes winter in Sheppey 867 to 880 Danes colonise Northumbria, Mercia and E. Anglia, making the Danelaw 886 Treaty of Alfred with Danes makes Watling St. boundary of Danelaw
		900
Building of Churches such as Earls Barton, Bradford on Avon Development of fine English handwriting and illuminations of Winchester School 987-98 Aelfric's *Homilies*, *Colloquy* and *Saints' Lives*	Building of fortresses, Market regulations, Danish trade } encourage growth of towns	Continental marriage alliances of Edward and Athelstan Visits of Dunstan and Aethelwold to reformed monasteries of continent 973 Celtic Kings submit to Edgar at Chester 980 Renewal of Danish invasions 991 Battle of Maldon
		1000
1014 Wulfstan's *Sermon to the English* 1065 Westminster Abbey consecrated William I builds castles throughout England: e.g. White Tower of London Romanesque or 'Norman' period of architecture to end of 12th century ↓ New cathedrals: e.g. Canterbury, Winchester, Rochester, Durham William Rufus builds Westminster Hall	ca. 1000 First list of port and customs duties at Port of London Stimulus given to urban life by Norman Conquest (Domesday records 65 boroughs in 1066 to 90 in 1086)	1002 Ethelred marries Norman wife 1019 Cnut King of Denmark 1028 Cnut overlord of Norway 1066 Norwegians defeated at Stamford Bridge (Sept. 25) by English English defeated by Normans at Battle of Hastings (Oct. 14) 1085 Threat of Danish invasion 1087 William dies from injuries in war against King of France 1087-96 Normandy separated from England 1096 First Crusade

Kings and Great Men	Government	Religion
1100 Henry I	Introduction of Exchequer technique in central Treasury under Roger of Salisbury	Many houses of Austin canons founded
1135 Stephen	Agents of central government hold financial and judicial inquiries in the shires 1141-53 Civil War between Stephen and Maud	1128 Coming of Cistercian monks to England 1136 Stephen allows English Church free contact with Rome 1138 Theobald archbishop of Canterbury 1141 Clergy at Winchester reject Stephen and choose Maud as ruler of England
1154 Henry II	1166 Inquiry into obligations of military tenants 1166 *Assize of Clarendon* asserts royal justice in criminal matters and introduces systematic visitation of shires by royal justices for administrative control and civil and criminal justice 1170 Inquiry into local administration 1176 Establishment of permanent central body of royal judges 1180 Ranulf Glanvill Chief Justice till 1190 1191 Barons take combined judicial action against aggressive minister in Richard's absence	1162 Becket archbishop of Canterbury 1164 Becket opposes Henry's proposals for dealing with criminous clerks and leaves England 1170 Murder of Becket on return to England 1172-76 Henry accepts appellate authority of Pope in church law and exemption of clergy from criminal law
1189 Richard I		
1199 John 1200	1213 Archbishop exacts promise to uphold law and justice from John 1215 *Magna Carta* sealed at Runnymede; but repudiated by John 1216 Henry III's counsellors re-issue Magna Carta 1234 Henry tries and abandons experiment at autocracy Steady advance in organization of finance and justice 1254 First presence of representatives of shires at a parliament 1258 Parliament at Oxford; experiment of baronial government begins 1263 Experiment fails; fighting begins 1265 Representatives of towns attend de Montfort's parliament. De Montfort killed at Evesham	1206 John refuses to accept Stephen Langton as archbishop. Quarrel with Innocent III lasting till 1213 1213 John does homage to Pope for England 1221 Coming of friars to England 1226 to 1256 General complaints of heavy Papal taxation and of appointments of foreigners to English benefices by Pope 1255 Henry promises large sum to Pope in return for crown of Sicily for his son, but is unable to pay (1257)
1216 Henry III		

Vertical span labels (left column): John of Salisbury 1115-80 · Hugh of Lincoln 1155-1200 · *ca.* 1145-1219 · William Marshal · 1200-53 · Robert Grosseteste 1214-94 · Simon de Montfort —1265 · Roger Bacon 1214-94 · Henry of Bracton —1268

ART AND LETTERS	COMMERCE AND INDUSTRY	EXTERNAL RELATIONS
	Organization of Gilds Merchant in many towns ↓ Advance in cloth weaving |	1117-20 Henry at war with King of France, and Counts of Anjou and Flanders
History of William of Malmesbury		1128 Henry marries his daughter Maud to Geoffrey of Anjou
Geoffrey of Monmouth's *History of the Britons* *The Rule of Anchoresses* Household of Archbishop Theobald a centre of learning 1149 Vacarius lectures at Oxford William of Newbury, Roger Hoveden, and many other historians writing	1130 (onwards) An increasing number of towns purchase charters of liberties from Kings	1152 Henry of Anjou and Normandy marries Eleanor of Aquitaine
Lives of Becket by Grim, John of Salisbury, etc.		1173 League of Henry's sons, the Kings of France and Scotland, and the Count of Flanders with Anglo-Norman barons
1177 *Dialogue of the Exchequer* 1180-90 Glanvill's *The Laws of England* Walter Map, *Courtiers' Trifles* Giraldus Cambrensis (1146-1220), *Conquest of Ireland, Journey through Wales, Autobiography*, etc.	1188 Direct taxation of personal property introduced in shape of crusading tax 1191 First Mayor of London	1190 Richard goes on Third Crusade
	Steady progress in production and export of wool Mayors of towns mentioned Improvements in agricultural techniques and estate management	1200 1204 Loss of Normandy 1211 Pope authorizes Philip of France to enforce his sentence on John 1216 Louis of France invades England 1226 Loss of Poitou
'Sumer is icumen in' 1232 First mention of university at Cambridge 1220-58 Building of Salisbury Cathedral *ca.* 1254 Bracton's *Laws of England* 1217-59 Matthew Paris writing 1265 *Song of Lewes*		1259 Treaty between Louis of France and Henry, recognizing *status quo*

KINGS AND GREAT MEN	GOVERNMENT	RELIGION
1272 Edward I	1268 *Statute of Marlborough* re-enacts Baronial reforms 1275-90 Great Statutes of Edward I 1297 Edward agrees under pressure not to levy taxes without consent	1296 Clergy forbidden by Pope to pay taxes to King; but prohibition withdrawn soon
1300 1307 Edward II	1310 Thomas of Lancaster and other barons draw up *Ordinances* to limit powers of king 1322 Execution of Thomas of Lancaster 1325 Last Parliament without representatives	1307 Protest in parliament against papal appointments to benefices
1327 Edward III	1327 Deposition of Edward II approved in Parliament 1328-89 Development by trial and error of office of Justice of the Peace	The English Mystics flourishing: Richard Rolle 1290-1349; Walter Hilton 1310-96; Julian of Norwich 1343-1443
	1337-41 Edward III tries and abandons experiment of bureaucratic autocracy	1351-93 Anti-papal statutes
	1362-73 House of Commons control of customs established 1376 Good Parliament: impeachment of ministers	1371 Foundation of London Charterhouse
1377 Richard II	1377 First mention of Speaker of House of Commons 1388 'Merciless' Parliament tries King's ministers	1377-78 Wyclif tried for heresy
	1397-98 Richard's last parliament sentences his opponents and passes severe treason law	1398 Concordat of Richard II with Pope (abandoned by Henry IV)
1399 Henry IV	1399 Deposition of Richard II approved by Henry's first Parliament	

Art and Letters	Commerce and Industry	External Relations
1269 Rebuilding of Westminster Abbey Church completed	1275 Agreement between Edward and wool merchants as to customs	1277 Invasion of Wales 1284 Annexation of Wales 1291 Edward presides at Scottish succession tribunal 1289 Edward defeats Scots at Falkirk and attempts to annex Scotland
	Development of trading monopoly of Merchants of Staple Development of craft gilds	1300 1314 Scots defeat English at Bannockburn 1328 Edward recognizes independence of Scotland
1331-7 Appearance of 'Perpendicular' style at Gloucester Abbey		1333 French help Scots against England 1337 Edward III claims French throne
	1347 Black Death	1346 Victory at Crecy followed by capture of Calais
ca. 1350 *The Cloud of Unknowing* *Winner and Waster*	1349 Ordinance of Labourers 1353 Ordinance of the Staple destroys monopoly of Staplers	
1360-80 Wyclif at Oxford 1362 English to be used in law courts		1356 French king taken prisoner at Poitiers
1378-9 William of Wykeham founds Winchester and New College	1381 Peasants' Revolt	1369 Aquitaine revolts against English rule Series of English losses in France. Only three ports left in 1374
1384-90 *The Canterbury Tales* 1362-92 *Piers Plowman* in different versions English translation of New Testament	1388 Statute of Cambridge: first vagrancy law	
1398-9 Westminster Hall restored		

KINGS AND GREAT MEN	GOVERNMENT	RELIGION
1400	1403 Revolt of Percies	1401 Statute for burning heretics
1413 Henry V	1407 Commons successfully assert special concern with taxation	1410 Proposals in Parliament to take away Church property
		1413-17 Threats of Lollard rising
1422 Henry VI		1414 Property of alien priories taken into King's hands by act of parliament
	1430 Election of county representatives to be by 40-shilling freeholders only	1415 Foundation of Syon Abbey
	1453 Insanity of King: Richard of York appointed protector	
	1455 Beginning of civil war	
1461 Edward IV	1461 Parliament accepts Edward IV	
	1471 Brief restoration of Henry VI followed by his murder	
1483 Edward VI (two months)		
1483 Richard III	1485 Parliament accepts Henry VII	
1485 Henry VII	1487 Judicial Committee of Council authorized to try lawless by summary procedure	
1500		
1509 Henry VIII	1515 Wolsey Lord Chancellor	1515 Wolsey Cardinal (legate 1518)
		1521 Henry VIII given title of Defender of the Faith by Pope for book against Luther
		1527 Henry seeks dissolution of marriage to Katharine
	1529-36 Reformation Parliament carries through separation from Rome by statute	1529 Fall of Wolsey: Katharine appeals to Rome
		1531 Clergy recognize Henry as 'Head of the Church'
		1532 Appeals to Rome forbidden by statute
		1533 Archbishop Cranmer annuls Henry's marriage to Katharine and upholds his marriage to Anne Boleyn
	1535 Act of Supremacy makes King Head of Church of England	1535 Execution of Fisher and More for denying royal headship of Church
		1536-39 Dissolution of monasteries
		1537 English Bible placed in churches
		1539 Act of Six articles upholds Catholic dogma
1547 Edward VI	1549 Parliament approves *The Book of Common Prayer*	
1553 Jane(13days)		1549 First Prayer Book in English
1553 Mary	1553-55 Mary's parliaments repeal Reformation Statutes	
	1554 Execution of Lady Jane Gray	
		1556-58 Many Protestants burnt, including Cranmer (1556)
1558 Elizabeth		

Names spanning the "Kings and Great Men" column (vertical):

- Thomas Wolsey 1475-1530
- Sir Thomas More 1478-1535
- Thomas Cromwell 1485-1540
- Stephen Gardiner 1483-1555
- Thomas Cranmer 1489-1556
- Reginald Pole 1500-1558

ART AND LETTERS	COMMERCE AND INDUSTRY	EXTERNAL RELATIONS
1412-20 Lydgate's *Troy Book* *Ballad of Agincourt* set to music by Dunstable, who dies 1453 Correspondence of: Pastons Plumptons Celys 1436 Margery Kempe's *Auto-biography* written 1436 *The Libel of English Policy*	Advancing Disin-tegration of Manorial System Growth of Cloth Man-ufacture and export	1400 1400 Rising of Owen Glen-dower in Wales 1415 Henry claims French crown; invades France and wins victory of Agincourt 1420 Henry recognized as heir to French king 1422 Normandy under English rule 1429 Joan of Arc leads resist-ance 1436 English lose Paris 1445 Henry VI marries Mar-garet of Anjou
1455 Peacock's *Repressor of over-much blaming of clergy* 1470 Fortescue *In praise of the Laws of Eng-land* 1470 *Morte d'Arthur* of Malory 1477-91 Caxton's press at Westminster	Increasing regulation of industry by statute 1496 Commercial treaty with Burgundy 1496 Henry VII licenses Cabot's voyage of dis-covery	1453 All French possessions except Calais lost 1474 Alliance of England and Burgundy 1492 Treaty with France 1492-6 Perkin Warbeck, Pre-tender to English throne, supported by Scotland and Burgundy. (Warbeck executed 1499)
1509 Hawes' *Pastime of Pleasure* 1516 More's *Utopia* 1524-30 Tyn-dales's translation of Bible 1531 Elyot's *Governor*	1505 Henry VII grants the Merchant Adventurers a charter Enclosure of arable land for purposes of sheep-raising increasing mark-edly	1500 1501 Marriage of Henry's eld-est son to Katharine of Aragon (later married to his second son Henry VIII) 1511-14 War with France 1513 Battle of Flodden 1514 Peace with France and Scotland 1522-25 War with France
1542 Hall's *Union of Lancaster and York* 1545 Ascham's *Toxophilus* 1552 Lindsay's *Three Estates* 1557 Tottel's *Songs and Son-ettes* printed, including poems by Wyatt and Surrey	Lands of dissolved mon-asteries acquired by Laymen 1549 Risings in protest against enclosures	1536 Legal Union with Wales; Welsh members in Eng-lish Parliament 1554 Marriage of Mary with Philip of Spain 1557 England goes to war with France 1558 Loss of Calais

(Canning of Bristol 1399-1474)

Skelton 1462-1529

Wyatt 1503-42

Surrey 1517-47

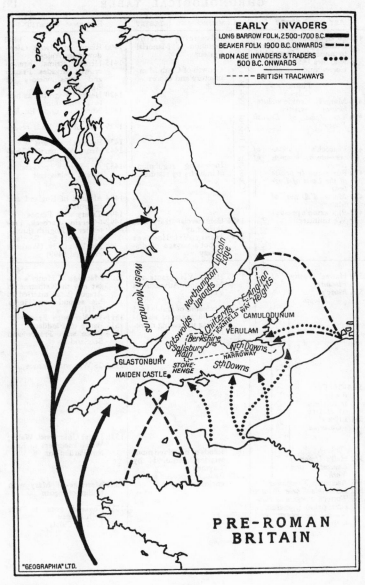

EARLY INVADERS
LONG BARROW FOLK, 2500-1700 B.C. ▬▬▬
BEAKER FOLK 1900 B.C. ONWARDS ▬ ▬ ▬
IRON AGE INVADERS & TRADERS
500 B.C. ONWARDS ●●●●●
▬ ▬ BRITISH TRACKWAYS

Welsh Mountains

Northampton Uplands

Lincoln Edge

E. Anglian Heights

Chilterns

Icknield Way

CAMULODUNUM

Cotswolds

Berkshire Dns

VERULAM

Salisbury Plain

Nth Downs

HARROWAY

GLASTONBURY

STONE-HENGE

Sth Downs

MAIDEN CASTLE

PRE-ROMAN
BRITAIN

"GEOGRAPHIA" LTD.

192

LINES OF ANGLO-SAXON INVASION INDICATED THUS

APPROXIMATE FRONTIERS OF KINGDOMS, 600 A.D.

APPROXIMATE FRONTIERS, 796 A.D.

BOUNDS OF DIRECT MERCIAN RULE AT DEATH OF OFFA, 796 A.D.

Iona

Tweed · Lindisfarne

NORTHUMBRIA

Tyne · Jarrow · Wearmouth

Tees · Whitby

Humber

Doncaster

LINDSEY · Lincoln

Chester

MERCIA

Lichfield

EAST ANGLIA

Tamworth

MIDDLE ANGLES · Ely

Cambridge

Waveney

Evesham

Stour

Gloucester

Cirencester

St Albans

ESSEX

Dorchester

London

KENT

Bath

WESSEX

Canterbury

Severn

Winchester

SUSSEX

OFFA'S DYKE

ERMINE ST.

RYKNIELD ST.

Trent

FOSSE WAY

WATLING

ICKNIELD WAY

BRITONS

ENGLAND
450-796 A.D.
UNDER THE BRETWEALDAS

"GEOGRAPHIA" LTD.

BOUNDARIES OF 886 — — — — —
BOUNDARY BETWEEN DANELAW AND
ALFRED'S KINGDOM IN 886 —·—·—·—
FORTRESSES CONSTRUCTED BY ALFRED & ●WILTON
HIS CHILDREN IN DANISH WARS
BOUNDARIES OF ENGLISH SHIRES IN 1066 ....

STRATHCLYDE

NORTHUMBRIA

GALLOWAY

CUMBRIA

Tees

York

Dee

Grimsby   Humber

RUNCORN

EDDISBURY   Lincoln
CHESTER

Derby
STAFFORD   Nottingham

DANELAW

WELSH

TAMWORTH   Stamford   Norwich

CHIRBURY   WATLING   Leicester   Ouse   Thetford

Northampton

WARWICK   Cambridge

WORCESTER   TOWCESTER   BEDFORD   Ipswich

GLOUCESTER   HERTFORD   WITHAM

Wantage   OXFORD   MALDON

DORCHESTER
CRICKLADE   WALLINGFD   London
Chippenham   Sheppey
Thames   SOUTHWARK

BATH
EDINGTON
×878

WATCHET   WILTON   WINCHESTER

Athelney   LEWES   1066   HASTINGS
×   Pevensey

EXETER   WAREHAM   CHICHESTER
BRIDPORT   DORCHESTER
CHRISTCHURCH

ENGLAND
886-1066 A.D.
UNDER THE
WEST SAXON KINGS

"GEOGRAPHIA" LTD.

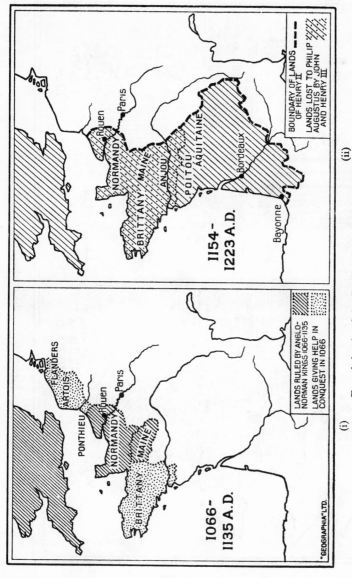

French lands of the English Kings 1066-1558

(i)

1066–1135 A.D.

FLANDERS
ARTOIS
PONTHIEU
Rouen
Paris
NORMANDY
MAINE
BRITTANY

LANDS RULED BY ANGLO-NORMAN KINGS 1066-1135
LANDS GIVING HELP IN CONQUEST IN 1066

"GEOGRAPHIA" LTD.

(ii)

1154–1223 A.D.

Rouen
Paris
NORMANDY
MAINE
BRITTANY
ANJOU
POITOU
AQUITAINE
Bordeaux
Bayonne

BOUNDARY OF LANDS OF HENRY II
LANDS LOST TO PHILIP AUGUSTUS BY JOHN AND HENRY III

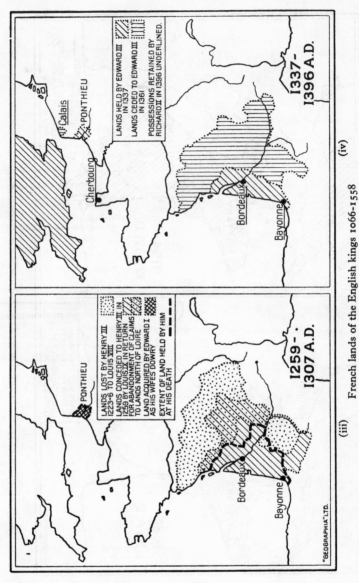

1337-1396 A.D.

LANDS HELD BY EDWARD III IN 1337
LANDS CEDED TO EDWARD III IN 1361
POSSESSIONS RETAINED BY RICHARD II IN 1396 UNDERLINED.

Calais
PONTHIEU
Cherbourg
Bordeaux
Bayonne

(iv)

1259-1307 A.D.

LANDS LOST BY HENRY III 1223-6 TO LOUIS VIII
LANDS CONCEDED TO HENRY III IN 1259 BY LOUIS IX IN RETURN FOR ABANDONMENT OF CLAIMS TO LANDS NORTH OF LOIRE
LAND ACQUIRED BY EDWARD I AS HIS WIFE'S DOWRY
EXTENT OF LAND HELD BY HIM AT HIS DEATH

PONTHIEU
Bordeaux
Bayonne

"GEOGRAPHIA" LTD.

(iii)   French lands of the English kings 1066-1558

196

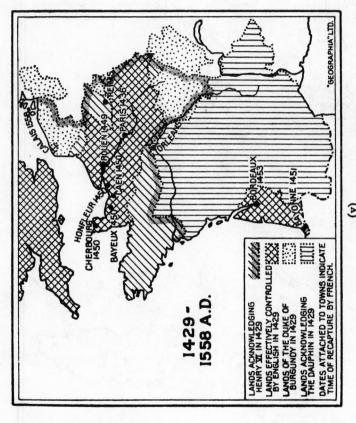

1429 – 1558 A.D.

CALAIS 1558

REIMS
ROUEN 1449
PARIS 1436
HONFLEUR
CHERBOURG
1450
BAYEUX 1450
CAEN 1450
ORLEANS

BORDEAUX
1453
BAYONNE 1451

"GEOGRAPHIA" LTD.

LANDS ACKNOWLEDGING
HENRY VI IN 1429

LANDS EFFECTIVELY CONTROLLED
BY ENGLISH IN 1429

LANDS OF THE DUKE OF
BURGUNDY IN 1429

LANDS ACKNOWLEDGING
THE DAUPHIN IN 1429

DATES ATTACHED TO TOWNS INDICATE
TIME OF RECAPTURE BY FRENCH.

(v)

French lands of the English kings 1066-1558

197

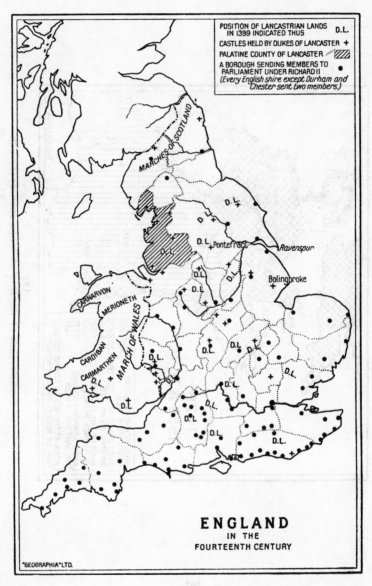

POSITION OF LANCASTRIAN LANDS
IN 1399 INDICATED THUS   **D.L.**
CASTLES HELD BY DUKES OF LANCASTER   **+**
PALATINE COUNTY OF LANCASTER
A BOROUGH SENDING MEMBERS TO
PARLIAMENT UNDER RICHARD II   **•**
*(Every English shire except Durham and
Chester sent two members.)*

MARCHES OF SCOTLAND

D. L.

D. L. Pontefract

Ravenspur

Bolingbroke

CARNARVON
MERIONETH

CARDIGAN
CARMARTHEN

MARCH OF WALES

D. L.

D. L.

D. L.

D. L.

D. L.

D. L.

D. L.

D. L.

D. L.

ENGLAND
IN THE
FOURTEENTH CENTURY

"GEOGRAPHIA" LTD.

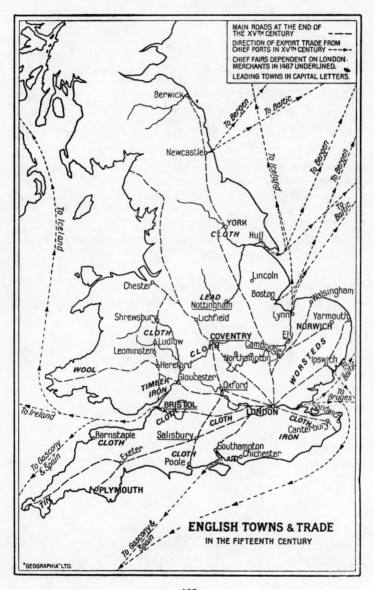

MAIN ROADS AT THE END OF
THE XVᵀᴴ CENTURY

DIRECTION OF EXPORT TRADE FROM
CHIEF PORTS IN XVᵀᴴ CENTURY

CHIEF FAIRS DEPENDENT ON LONDON·
MERCHANTS IN 1487 UNDERLINED.

LEADING TOWNS IN CAPITAL LETTERS.

To Bergen

To Baltic

To Iceland

To Bergen

To Bergen

To Baltic

To Iceland

Berwick

Newcastle

YORK
CLOTH
Hull

Chester

Lincoln
Boston

LEAD
Nottingham
Lichfield

Shrewsbury

Lynn
Walsingham
Yarmouth
NORWICH

CLOTH
Ludlow

COVENTRY
Cambridge
Ely

Leominster

CLOTH
Northampton

WORSTEDS
Ipswich

WOOL
Hereford
Gloucester
Oxford

TIMBER
IRON

To Baltic

To Bruges

BRISTOL

LONDON

Sandwich

To Ireland

CLOTH
CLOTH
CLOTH
IRON
Canterbury

Barnstaple
CLOTH
Salisbury

To Gascony
& Spain

Exeter
CLOTH
Poole
Southampton
Chichester

TIN
PLYMOUTH

To Gascony &
Spain

ENGLISH TOWNS & TRADE
IN THE FIFTEENTH CENTURY

"GEOGRAPHIA" LTD.

199

INDEX

70 71 72 73   12 11 10 9 8 7 6

hARPER ✦ τORChBOOKS

American Studies: General

CARL N. DEGLER: Out of Our Past: *The Forces that Shaped Modern America*   CN/2
ROBERT L. HEILBRONER: The Limits of American Capitalism   TB/1305
JOHN HIGHAM, Ed.: The Reconstruction of American History   TB/1068
JOHN F. KENNEDY: A Nation of Immigrants. *Illus. Revised and Enlarged. Introduction by Robert F. Kennedy*   TB/1118
GUNNAR MYRDAL: An American Dilemma: *The Negro Problem and Modern Democracy. Introduction by the Author.*
          Vol. I TB/1443;   Vol. II TB/1444
GILBERT OSOFSKY, Ed.: The Burden of Race: *A Documentary History of Negro-White Relations in America*   TB/1405
ARNOLD ROSE: The Negro in America: *The Condensed Version of Gunnar Mydral's An American Dilemma*   TB/3048

American Studies: Colonial

BERNARD BAILYN: The New England Merchants in the Seventeenth Century   TB/1149
ROBERT E. BROWN: Middle-Class Democracy and Revolution in Massachusetts, 1691–1780. *New Introduction by Author*   TB/1413
JOSEPH CHARLES: The Origins of the American Party System   TB/1049

American Studies: The Revolution to 1900

GEORGE M. FREDRICKSON: The Inner Civil War: *Northern Intellectuals and the Crisis of the Union*   TB/1358
WILLIAM W. FREEHLING: Prelude to Civil War: *The Nullification Controversy in South Carolina, 1816-1836*   TB/1359
HELEN HUNT JACKSON: A Century of Dishonor: *The Early Crusade for Indian Reform.* ‡ *Edited by Andrew F. Rolle*   TB/3063
RICHARD B. MORRIS, Ed.: Alexander Hamilton and the Founding of the Nation. *New Introduction by the Editor*   TB/1448
RICHARD B. MORRIS: The American Revolution Reconsidered   TB/1363
GILBERT OSOFSKY, Ed.: Puttin' On Ole Massa: *The Slave Narratives of Henry Bibb, William Wells Brown, and Solomon Northup* ‡   TB/1432

American Studies: The Twentieth Century

WILLIAM E. LEUCHTENBURG: Franklin D. Roosevelt and the New Deal: 1932-1940. † *Illus.*   TB/3025
WILLIAM E. LEUCHTENBURG, Ed.: The New Deal: *A Documentary History* +   HR/1354

Asian Studies

WOLFGANG FRANKE: China and the West: *The Cultural Encounter, 13th to 20th Centuries. Trans. by R. A. Wilson*   TB/1326
L. CARRINGTON GOODRICH: A Short History of the Chinese People. *Illus.*   TB/3015
BENJAMIN I. SCHWARTZ: Chinese Communism and the Rise of Mao   TB/1308

Economics & Economic History

PETER F. DRUCKER: The New Society: *The Anatomy of Industrial Order*   TB/1082
ROBERT L. HEILBRONER: The Great Ascent: *The Struggle for Economic Development in Our Time*   TB/3030
W. ARTHUR LEWIS: The Principles of Economic Planning. *New Introduction by the Author*°   TB/1436

Historiography and History of Ideas

J. BRONOWSKI & BRUCE MAZLISH: The Western Intellectual Tradition: *From Leonardo to Hegel*   TB/3001
WILHELM DILTHEY: Pattern and Meaning in History: *Thoughts on History and Society.*° *Edited with an Intro. by H. P. Rickman*   TB/1075
J. H. HEXTER: More's Utopia: *The Biography of an Idea. Epilogue by the Author*   TB/1195
ARTHUR O. LOVEJOY: The Great Chain of Being: *A Study of the History of an Idea*   TB/1009

History: Medieval

F. L. GANSHOF: Feudalism   TB/1058
DENYS HAY: The Medieval Centuries °   TB/1192
HENRY CHARLES LEA: A History of the Inquisition of the Middle Ages. ‖ *Introduction by Walter Ullmann*   TB/1456

---

† The New American Nation Series, edited by Henry Steele Commager and Richard B. Morris.
‡ American Perspectives series, edited by Bernard Wishy and William E. Leuchtenburg.
a History of Europe series, edited by J. H. Plumb.
§ The Library of Religion and Culture, edited by Benjamin Nelson.
‖ Researches in the Social, Cultural, and Behavioral Sciences, edited by Benjamin Nelson.
Σ Harper Modern Science Series, edited by James R. Newman.
° Not for sale in Canada.
+ Documentary History of the United States series, edited by Richard B. Morris.
# Documentary History of Western Civilization series, edited by Eugene C. Black and Leonard W. Levy.
Λ The Economic History of the United States series, edited by Henry David et al.
¶ European Perspectives series, edited by Eugene C. Black.
** Contemporary Essays series, edited by Leonard W Levy.
* The Stratum Series, edited by John Hale.

History: Renaissance & Reformation

JACOB BURCKHARDT: The Civilization of the Renaissance in Italy. *Introduction by Benjamin Nelson and Charles Trinkaus. Illus.* Vol. I TB/40; Vol. II TB/41

JOEL HURSTFIELD: The Elizabethan Nation TB/1312

ALFRED VON MARTIN: Sociology of the Renaissance. ° *Introduction by W. K. Ferguson* TB/1099

J. H. PARRY: The Establishment of the European Hegemony: 1415-1715: *Trade and Exploration in the Age of the Renaissance* TB/1045

History: Modern European

MAX BELOFF: The Age of Absolutism, 1660-1815 TB/1062

ALAN BULLOCK: Hitler, A Study in Tyranny. ° *Revised Edition. Illus.* TB/1123

JOHANN GOTTLIEB FICHTE: Addresses to the German Nation. *Ed. with Intro. by George A. Kelly* ¶ TB/1366

H. STUART HUGHES: The Obstructed Path: *French Social Thought in the Years of Desperation* TB/1451

JOHAN HUIZINGA: Dutch Cviilization in the 17th Century and Other Essays TB/1453

JOHN MCMANNERS: European History, 1789-1914: *Men, Machines and Freedom* TB/1419

FRANZ NEUMANN: Behemoth: *The Structure and Practice of National Socialism, 1933-1944* TB/1289

A. J. P. TAYLOR: From Napoleon to Lenin: *Historical Essays* ° TB/1268

H. R. TREVOR-ROPER: Historical Essays TB/1269

Philosophy

HENRI BERGSON: Time and Free Will: *An Essay on the Immediate Data of Consciousness* ° TB/1021

G. W. F. HEGEL: Phenomenology of Mind. ° ¶ *Introduction by George Lichtheim* TB/1303

H. J. PATON: The Categorical Imperative: *A Study in Kant's Moral Philosophy* TB/1325

MICHAEL POLANYI: Personal Knowledge: *Towards a Post-Critical Philosophy* TB/1158

LUDWIG WITTGENSTEIN: The Blue and Brown Books ° TB/1211

LUDWIG WITTGENSTEIN: Notebooks, 1914-1916 TB/1441

Political Science & Government

C. E. BLACK: The Dynamics of Modernization: *A Study in Comparative History* TB/1321

DENIS W. BROGAN: Politics in America. *New Introduction by the Author* TB/1469

KARL R. POPPER: The Open Society and Its Enemies *Vol. I: The Spell of Plato* TB/1101 *Vol. II: The High Tide of Prophecy: Hegel, Marx, and the Aftermath* TB/1102

CHARLES SCHOTTLAND, Ed.: The Welfare State ** TB/1323

JOSEPH A. SCHUMPETER: Capitalism, Socialism and Democracy TB/3008

PETER WOLL, Ed.: Public Administration and Policy: *Selected Essays* TB/1284

Psychology

LUDWIG BINSWANGER: Being-in-the-World: *Selected Papers.* ¶ *Trans. with Intro. by Jacob Needleman* TB/1365

MIRCEA ELIADE: Cosmos and History: *The Myth of the Eternal Return* § TB/2050

SIGMUND FREUD: On Creativity and the Unconscious: *Papers on the Psychology of Art, Literature, Love, Religion.* § *Intro. by Benjamin Nelson* TB/45

J. GLENN GRAY: The Warriors: *Reflections on Men in Battle. Introduction by Hannah Arendt* TB/1294

WILLIAM JAMES: Psychology: *The Briefer Course. Edited with an Intro. by Gordon Allport* TB/1034

Religion

TOR ANDRAE: Mohammed: *The Man and his Faith* TB/62

KARL BARTH: Church Dogmatics: *A Selection. Intro. by H. Hollwitzer. Ed. by G. W. Bromiley* TB/95

NICOLAS BERDYAEV: The Destiny of Man TB/61

MARTIN BUBER: The Prophetic Faith TB/73

MARTIN BUBER: Two Types of Faith: *Interpenetration of Judaism and Christianity* TB/75

RUDOLF BULTMANN: History and Eschatalogy: *The Presence of Eternity* TB/91

EDWARD CONZE: Buddhism: *Its Essence and Development. Foreword by Arthur Waley* TB/58

H. G. CREEL: Confucius and the Chinese Way TB/63

FRANKLIN EDGERTON, Trans. & Ed.: The Bhagavad Gita TB/115

M. S. ENSLIN: Christian Beginnings TB/5

M. S. ENSLIN: The Literature of the Christian Movement TB/6

HENRI FRANKFORT: Ancient Egyptian Religion: *An Interpretation* TB/77

IMMANUEL KANT: Religion Within the Limits of Reason Alone. *Introduction by Theodore M. Greene and John Silber* TB/67

GABRIEL MARCEL: Homo Viator: *Introduction to a Metaphysic of Hope* TB/397

H. RICHARD NIEBUHR: Christ and Culture TB/3

H. RICHARD NIEBUHR: The Kingdom of God in America TB/49

SWAMI NIKHILANANDA, Trans. & Ed.: The Upanishads TB/114

F. SCHLEIERMACHER: The Christian Faith. *Introduction by Richard R. Niebuhr.* Vol. I TB/108 Vol. II TB/109

Sociology and Anthropology

KENNETH B. CLARK: Dark Ghetto: *Dilemmas of Social Power. Foreword by Gunnar Myrdal* TB/1317

KENNETH CLARK & JEANNETTE HOPKINS: A Relevant War Against Poverty: *A Study of Community Action Programs and Observable Social Change* TB/1480

GARY T. MARX: Protest and Prejudice: *A Study of Belief in the Black Community* TB/1435

ROBERT K. MERTON, LEONARD BROOM, LEONARD S. COTTRELL, JR., Editors: Sociology Today: *Problems and Prospects* ¶ Vol. I TB/1173; Vol. II TB/1174

GILBERT OSOFSKY: Harlem: The Making of a Ghetto: *Negro New York, 1890-1930* TB/1381

PHILIP RIEFF: The Triumph of the Therapeutic: *Uses of Faith After Freud* TB/1360

GEORGE ROSEN: Madness in Society: *Chapters in the Historical Sociology of Mental Illness.* ¶ *Preface by Benjamin Nelson* TB/1337